2000
Sure-Fire Jokes
For Speakers

Also by Robert Orben

2000
Sure-Fire Jokes
For Speakers
THE ENCYCLOPEDIA
OF ONE-LINER COMEDY

Robert Orben

MAIN
STREET
BOOKS

DOUBLEDAY
NEW YORK LONDON TORONTO SYDNEY AUCKLAND

A MAIN STREET BOOK
PUBLISHED BY DOUBLEDAY
a division of Bantam Doubleday Dell Publishing Group, Inc.
1540 Broadway, New York, New York 10036

MAIN STREET BOOKS, DOUBLEDAY, and the portrayal of a
building with a tree are trademarks of Doubleday, a division of
Bantam Doubleday Dell Publishing Group, Inc.

This book was originally published under the
title *The Encyclopedia of One-Liner Comedy*

Library of Congress Cataloging-in-Publication Data
Orben, Robert.
    2000 sure-fire jokes for speakers.
    Originally published: The encyclopedia of one-liner
        comedy / Robert Orben. 1971.
    ISBN 0-385-23465-1 (pbk.)
    1. American wit and humor. 2. Public speaking—
Handbooks, manuals, etc. I. Title. II. Title:
Two thousand sure-fire jokes for speakers.
PN6162.O695   1986   818'.5402   85-25442

Copyright © 1966, 1967, 1968, 1971, 1986 by Robert Orben
ALL RIGHTS RESERVED
PRINTED IN THE UNITED STATES OF AMERICA

        11   12   10

Introduction

The one-liner joke is the essential element of today's comedy. Without it, most of the successful laugh makers in show business would stand mute. Take away one-liners and our most popular public speakers would have a much more difficult time bridging the distance between platform and audience. Remove these short, explosive bursts of humor—and the effervescence of our everyday conversation goes flat.

Any individual engaged in the task of communicating entertainment, ideas, or information is in a constant search for one-liners that are relevant today. Here, in THE ENCYCLOPEDIA OF ONE-LINERS COMEDY, are more than two thousand of these choice laugh morsels conveniently arranged by subject matter. They can be used as the mortar that holds together disparate elements of a speech or presentation. They are the bricks with which you can construct effective comedy talks. They are a warm calling card that introduces you to strangers as someone worth knowing. Above all, they are two thousand chunks of sure-fire laughter, ready and able to be put to instant use by the hip, the alert, and the aware in any business or profession.

Thomas Carlyle wrote: "No man who has once heartily and wholly laughed can be altogether irreclaimably bad." Here is your chance to spread goodness, light, and virtue throughout the world!

He's got to be kidding.

Yes. That's the whole idea of the book.

BOB ORBEN

2000
Sure-Fire Jokes
For Speakers

A

ADAM AND EVE

All the trouble in the Garden of Eden started when Eve bit into a piece of fruit. I had the same problem down in Mexico!

The Garden of Eden is where Adam and Eve went around topless down to their toes!

You remember Eve. The first woman who ever said: "I haven't got a thing to wear" and meant it!

You know what I can't understand? Here's Adam and Eve. He's incredibly handsome and she's indescribably beautiful. So where did all the ugly people come from?

And here are Adam and Eve living together in Paradise. You can tell it's Paradise. Not once does Eve ask Adam to take out the garbage!

When Adam bit into the apple, you could tell it was from the Tree of Knowledge. Adam looked at the apple, turned to Eve and said: "You call this dinner?"

I don't wanna complain, but if I were Adam in the Garden of Eden —and I put on a fig leaf to hide my nakedness—with my luck it'd be poison oak!

I've got nothing against women. I just happen to believe that old story that when God created Eve—the snake nudged Adam and said: "Well, there goes the neighborhood!"

As Adam once said to Eve: "Cain? Abel? What's wrong with Melvin?"

ADVERTISING

Now there's a special perfume for Madison Avenue junior executives who want to appear conscientious. It smells like fear.

Now there's a new protest sign for Madison Avenue: MAKE LOVE, NOT DEADLINES!

How's this for an idea? We put out a saccharine with the trade name Adversity—and William Shakespeare gives us the advertising slogan: "Sweet are the uses of Adversity!" . . . I get these headaches, but I'll be all right. . . .

You have to watch some of these advertising concepts. I know a girl who's convinced her living bra bit her!

I don't know why they call them unmentionables when you can't pick up a magazine without seeing a full page ad of them.

AIRLINES

I'm one of those weak stomach fliers. With me, UP, UP, AND AWAY is lunch!

There's a new outfit that calls itself the world's most fastidious airline. Under each wing it doesn't have wheels. It has a deodorant.

I saw a movie on a plane that was so good, nobody even noticed the crash!

You can always tell a car owner in an airplane. He's the one who, when they close the door—opens it again and slams it harder!

So we're flying along and the pilot said over the loudspeaker: "We're now flying over the Rocky Mountains." One of the passengers said: "Pardon me, sir, but I happen to be an astronomer and I can tell from the stars that we're now flying over the Mississippi River." So they opened the door and threw him out—'cause nobody likes a smart astronomer!

Did you hear about the drunk who saw the Flying Nun go by? He said: "I've heard of Economy Class but this is ridiculous!"

Now they're working on a plane that'll seat 490 people. And that's just in the washroom!

The plane is so big, it'll have twelve stewardesses and everything will be specialized. Three stewardesses will say: "Coffee?" Three will say: "Tea?" Three will say: "Milk?" And three will say: "No!"

"Personally, I don't believe in supersonic transports."
"Because you're conservative?"
"No. Because I lisp!"

AIR POLLUTION

Did you hear about the new motto of the smog prevention bureau? *Cherchez la fume?*

I can remember when "Smoke Gets in Your Eyes" was a song instead of a weather report!

I'll tell you how bad the smog is. I know an artist who paints what he sees. Hasn't painted in three years!

For those of you who have never seen the Los Angeles air—you know how Ed Norton works in the sewer? Out here we all do!

A little song dedicated to the smog: "When your hair has turned to silver and your eyes have turned to red."

I didn't realize how bad the smog was until they started making freeway signs in braille!

I know a fella who married a girl so ugly, he only kisses her during smog alerts!

Air pollution is a little different from the weather. Everybody talks about it and everybody does something about it. They contribute to it!

A scientist wants to put cities under glass. How do you like that? New York could start out a city and wind up a pheasant!

Can you imagine an entire city under glass? We'd never have to worry about cold or rain or snow again. Just little kids with rocks!

ANXIETY

Right now, things are so confused—I know a Ouija Board that just shrugs!

Nervous? I feel like a pizza on the way to Jackie Gleason!

I won't say how insecure people are getting, but Dial-A-Prayer just added two more numbers!

Personally, I never have any problems in coping with the realities of life. I just follow those four magic words a wise old Indian guru once taught to me: WHEN IN DOUBT—CRUMBLE!

Insecurity is reading about a fella getting arrested at the Y.W.C.A. for being a Peeping Tom—and it's your psychiatrist.

I just had a terrible nightmare. I dreamt I owned a laundry in BERKELEY!

Everybody's shook up these days. Teen-agers are upset because they're living in a world dominated by nuclear weapons—and adults are upset because they're living in a world dominated by teen-agers!

APARTMENTS

I live in one of those apartment houses that doesn't allow children, and they really mean it. One of the tenants is now in her sixteenth month!

I had a terrible argument with the landlord. He called my wife a dumb blonde. She's not a blonde!

I won't say what kind of an apartment we've got, but you know those ads that claim you can make a fortune growing mushrooms in your cellar? We could do it in our living room!

ARMY

I could never understand these girls who write Dear John letters. What a crazy thing to be in love with!

This platoon was taking a few-minutes break to wolf down a meal of lukewarm, grayish-looking stew. As a sergeant poked at it with a spoon, he said: "You know something? If my wife could see this, would she be mad!" The soldier next to him asked: "Why would she be mad?" The sergeant took another look at the limpid stew and said: "I think it's her recipe!"

Tell me, what does an Army cook do when he gets discharged? Let's face it. Every recipe he knows ends up with: SERVES 2000!

There's this about the Army—you never have to decide on what to wear.

You'd be surprised how many fellas join the services for romantic reasons. Like I know a guy who joined the Army to forget his girl friend. Then he joined the Air Force to forget the Army!

Frankly, I don't look on it as the armed forces. To me, it's more like a prep school for the American Legion.

The Pentagon is trying all kinds of things to get teen-agers interested in the Army. Like they just came up with a .45-caliber guitar.

ART

Do you realize if Toulouse Lautrec were alive today, he wouldn't be a painter? He'd be a chauffeur in a Volkswagen!

What a sensational idea for an art school. You don't paint the nude models—you trace them!

If you think Whistler's father is forgotten—how about the chef for the "Last Supper?"

Did you hear about the Texas art connoisseur who saw Rembrandt's "The Night Watch" and said: "I like that. I like that very much! It has character, depth, understanding, perception. If you have one in green, I'll buy it!"

You know what I admire about Rembrandt? He was the first artist to paint it like it is!

Rembrandt had a very unusual style. He put more people in shadow than the light man at a burlesque house.

Show me a hippie sculptor who works in a basement—and I'll show you a dirty, low-down chiseler!

I was reading a book about Michelangelo—an Italian painter who took seven years to finish a ceiling. And they couldn't say anything because he was Union!

Michelangelo spent seven years painting the ceiling of the Sistine Chapel. He didn't mind the seven years so much. What bugged him was when they asked for a second coat!

And as luck would have it—Michelangelo finished his masterpiece, climbed down from the scaffolding, and the very first person he ran into was his mother-in-law. She looked up at the ceiling, looked at him, and said: "From this you make a living?"

Did you ever see that painting of the "Mona Lisa?" It always reminds me of a reporter listening to a politician.

Modern art is when you buy a picture to cover a hole in the wall—and then decide the hole looks better.

A sad thing happened at the art museum yesterday. They replaced that statue of "The Thinker"—with a computer.

ATOMIC BOMBS

Between us and them, there must be 60,000 nuclear warheads around the world. If they're ever used, it'll be the first time in history a planet was ever mugged!

You can't even take refuge in religion. How can you gather at the river when it's no longer there?

Sixty thousand nuclear warheads! Remember that song: "He's got the whole world in his hands?" If I were Him, I'd let go!

Fortunately, my wife puts all of these things in perspective. She said: "Can you imagine if all 60,000 nuclear warheads went off at the same time?" I said: "Yes?" She said. "Just my luck—I'd be baking a sponge cake!"

I love the way we call something that's the equivalent of 20,000 tons of TNT—low-yield. It may be low-yield, but it ain't exactly a burp either!

You drop a 20,000 ton atom bomb on Greenwich Village and it'd be raining limp wrists for three days!

They say the Red Chinese are going to set off another nuclear explosion. Wouldn't it be funny if the Chinese don't even have an atom bomb? It's the Jolly Green Giant eating a Hungarian dinner?

Most experts feel the Red Chinese don't have an effective means of delivery. We have a Post Office with the same problem.

B

BABIES

Feeding a baby is simple if you remember one thing: Everything that goes into a baby's mouth has to be boiled. Which is why bottle-feeding has become so popular.

Babies are very delicate. For instance, if you pick one up, you have to hold the head to keep from breaking his neck. And when they become teen-agers—you have to hold your temper to keep from doing likewise.

Even the young kids are starting to rebel. I heard a red-haired father talking to his blond-haired baby. He said: "Whose little boy are you? Whose little boy are you?" The kid looked up at him and said: "You're beginning to wonder too?"

Everything's so modern these days. Like baby buggies. They all have air-conditioning, stereo, bucket seats. I saw one yesterday—had a fastback. Not the buggy—the baby.

Now I know why they say: "Hold the head!" It's the safest part!

And for you do-it-yourself fans, it's very easy to make a baby buggy. Tickle its toes!

But you should be very careful how you treat a baby 'cause it can influence the rest of his life. Like my mother used to hire people to take me out in my baby buggy—and I've been pushed for money ever since!

BACHELORS

It's wonderful to be a bachelor. To eat home-cooked meals but have your choice of cooks.

I know a bachelor who's so civic-minded, he rents a kid just to go to P.T.A. meetings!

I won't say I've got bad luck with women, but I think I have one of those whistles only dogs can hear.

I'm so celibate I read *Playboy* for the ads! . . . Last week three monasteries made me an offer!

BASEBALL

I just found out why they call that ball club the Angels. No matter what a pitcher throws at them, they never hit back!

Did you hear about the (local team) outfielder who went home; caught Hell from his wife—and dropped it?

I'll say this about the (local team)—they're non-violent. One of them hasn't hit anything in weeks.

I don't wanna say anything about this ball club, but yesterday going into the ninth, they had a no-hitter going for them. Not the pitcher—the batters!

We're becoming a nation of watchers. Nowadays you give a kid a baseball bat and they wanna know if instructions come with it!

Have you seen the latest? A get-well card for people who bet on the Expos!

You've heard of baseball widows? We live next door to one. She hit her husband with a bat!

On February 1, 1865, President Lincoln signed a document that abolished slavery in the United States. As I understand it, it covered everybody but professional baseball players.

Baseball games are where you go to eat peanuts and crackerjacks—

and if you don't care if you never come back, that's perfect 'cause there are terrible traffic jams in the parking lot!

I was in one baseball parking lot so long, the people on the way in were football fans!

They say baseball is our national pastime—and what the Montreal Expos play is pretty popular too!

The one nice thing about being an Expo fan is everybody knows the troubles you've seen.

You know who believes in birth control? The (cellar baseball team)! They haven't scored in weeks!

BIRTH CONTROL

No wonder birth control is such a problem. Look at the phrase itself—"birth control." Doesn't make sense. It's nine months before that you need the control!

Now they've come up with the subtlest birth-control device of them all—sticky zippers!

Have you heard the latest? Birth-control pills for people with their money in Wall Street.

There's only one problem with birth control. Who's gonna pay off all the debts the government is running up?

Have you noticed how sneaky birth-control groups are getting? One of them just put out a bumper sticker: HELP STAMP OUT P.T.A.S!

Planned Parenthood is a very confusing name. It infers that kids have a choice.

Planned Parenthood is when the kids tell you what time you can use the car.

Did you hear about the bookstore that has a special section of birth-control books—with a sign over it saying: BETTER READ THAN BRED!

BOOKS

In many ways, the Bible is a surprisingly modern story. Like Noah in the Ark? It took him forty days to find a place to park!

You remember the story of the Ark. The ship that carried a male and female of every living creature on earth. I think it was the last cruise ship that was ever evenly matched!

Then it rained for forty days and forty nights. I've had vacations like that myself!

You know what I like about the story of Sodom and Gomorrah in the Bible? It comes right out and names names!

I was just reading that new best seller: *Is Air-Conditioning Making American Women Frigid?*

I was reading that book *Sex Before Twenty*. Personally, I don't like audiences.

BREAD

I just bought two loaves of bread at the supermarket. Fortunately, I had a co-signer.

Have you noticed what's been happening to the price of bread? Now you know why Marie Antoinette said: "Let them eat cake!" It's cheaper!

One store is advertising: "CRACKED WHEAT—49¢ A LOAF." I got news. Anyone who pays 49¢ for a loaf of bread, is more cracked than the wheat!

For years they've been selling bread that's labeled "ENRICHED!" And now we know who they mean—the baker!

I won't say how much money is being made, but you know THE BUTCHER, THE BAKER, THE CANDLESTICK MAKER? The Candlestick Maker is on welfare and the other two are in Beverly Hills.

And there's no such thing as a small loaf of bread any more. They're all huge! 'Cause they're giving you something for your money they never gave you before—air! This morning I cut open a loaf and thought I had a flat!

Do you realize they now have a chemical that makes bread last up to six months? I can remember when bread was enriched. Now it's embalmed!

And the fantastic part of it is you eat this bread and it lasts another six months. In your stomach!

But bread today has everything. They've added Vitamins A, B, C, D, and E—not to mention the ever-popular riboflavin. In fact, bread today is so crowded, they have to leave one thing out—flavor!

It's kinda hard to describe what bread tastes like these days. I think the reason peanut butter sticks to the roof of your mouth is it doesn't wanna get too close to the bread!

BUSINESS

They talk about American efficiency, yet the secretary always answers the phone, and most of the time it's for her boss.

The trouble with women in the business world, if you treat them like men, they get mad. And if you treat them like women, your wife gets mad.

I just heard a weird conversation. It went something like this:
"Frankly, I'd say Sam lacks good business judgment."
"Why do you say that?"
"Well, he did buy that Edsel agency."
"Lots of people bought Edsel agencies."
"Last week?"

You have to be imaginative in the business world. Like I know an insurance salesman who makes $500,000 a year just because of one little innovation—coed physicals!

It's easy to tell inventory from money. Money's the stuff you can get rid of.

Did you hear about the diaper maker that added a fiendishly clever sideline—a factory-second Pill?

My grandfather was one of the men who built America. Like in 1912, he came up with a slogan: PROGRESS IS OUR MOST IMPORTANT PRODUCT. There was only one trouble. He made horse cars.

I'm busier than a fella wearing bifocals at a burlesque show!

BUS TRAVEL

I once traveled coast-to-coast on a bus. Three thousand miles and four rest stops! . . . I can still hear my kidneys singing: WE SHALL OVERCOME!

I love that name "rest stop." After 4½ hours of hopping on one foot, you'd be tired too!

I don't know who plans the distance between rest stops for the bus company, but I think it's the Marquis de Sade!

And the food they serve at these rest stops! If they served this food to a condemned man before he walked that last mile—he'd be looking forward to the trip!

C

CALIFORNIA

I had a terrible dream about California last night—that George Murphy and Ronald Reagan got out of politics, and someone yelled: "Strike the state!"

You gotta admit one thing about California. It's chic! Where else can you see a fella robbing a bank with a stocking pulled over his head—and it's patterned?

You can't believe how style conscious Californians are. Have you heard the latest—a mini-shroud?

I love California. Any state that has a cash-and-carry mortuary can't be all bad.

You know what I like about California? Anything goes! Yesterday, I saw two hearses drag racing!

There are some wild things going on out in California. I met a fella who was growing Bonsai Marijuana for short hippies.

You gotta admit Los Angeles means well. Where else can you listen to a gypsy violinist—in a Chinese restaurant?

Beverly Hills is so exclusive—this is the only town in America where Chicken Delight has an unlisted number!

And Beverly Hills is so rich. It's the first time I ever saw a Salvation Army Band with a string section!

You remember Sunset Strip—where the Unneat Meet to Bleat!

A lot of people make fun of the kids on Sunset Strip but not me. They're the hope of America. I'm learning Russian right now!

CAR

Now there's a group called the O.O.A.A.A. It's for people who get a flat tire two days after their membership expires!

Have you noticed how the new cars are just like eating radishes? One outfit comes up with a good idea and the rest keep repeating it!

You always hear about your friendly neighborhood car dealer, but I never realized how friendly he was until he sold me this car. He said: "I have just one thing to say before you get in that car." I said: "What's that?" He said: "Don't get in that car!"

If you really want to drive one of those rent-a-car outfits out of their minds—rent a car in Los Angeles, then back it up to San Francisco!

I'm with one of those auto insurance companies that question everything. I think I've got $50 Debatable.

I once knew a woman who accomplished the unbelievable. Got seven miles to a gallon driving one of those little sports cars. Nobody could figure it out until they watched her drive. First thing she did when she got in the car, was pull the choke all the way out, so she could hang her purse on it!

Did you hear about the fella with a wife and three teen-agers who went out and bought a car for his own private, personal, exclusive use? He calls it a Pop Rod!

I don't wanna brag, but I have a Rolls. Not a Rolls-Royce. A Rolls. All it does is go downhill!

This car is so old the clock on the dashboard is a sun dial!

But it's a wonderful car. Comes with two shock absorbers—me and my wife!

I don't want to say anything about this car, but if I used it to buy a skateboard, I'd be trading up!

CAR ACCESSORIES

Personally, I would never own a car that didn't have a padded dashboard. Let's face it. Do you realize what would happen if your head hit that dashboard and it wasn't padded? Who's gonna buy a car with a bent clock?

And it's amazing the electronic gadgets you can buy. One car has a device that not only tells you when you're coming to a radar trap—but on the screen in the cop's car, it makes the blips into a . . . (THUMB YOUR NOSE)!

Personally, I don't believe in those bumper stickers that say: SUPPORT YOUR LOCAL POLICE If there's one thing I can't stand, it's a drunken cop!

I think they oughta do something about those risqué bumper stickers. I mean, I don't mind for myself—but my car is only six years old!

I just saw the craziest bumper sticker. It said: SUPPORT AMERICAN LABOR. BAN THE PILL!

CAR ADVERTISING

My favorite cars are convertibles—especially the way they advertise them. They always show this long, sleek, red convertible being driven by a blonde in a bikini. You know what it reminds me of? A Welcome Wagon in Peyton Place!

Have you been reading the ads on the new cars? The way they

describe them as throbbing, racy beauties with sleek, lean bodies! You don't know whether to take them to your garage or a motel!

I figure the automobile industry would be in good shape if the same people who wrote their ads, built their cars!

CAR PRICES

Every year Detroit tries to add something new to cars. Sometimes they add it to the engine. Sometimes they add it to the body. This year they're adding it to the price tag—a hundred dollars!

They keep talking about crime in the streets. To me that's the price of new cars!

I paid $4800 for a car but it gets me where I'm going—the poorhouse!

I can remember when $150 was the down payment on a new car. Now it's the sales tax!

Nowadays, if you want to buy a $5000 car, it's easy. Buy a $3000 car on time!

I bought a car on time and it's a fascinating experience. Our atom bombs should be as well hidden as car payment interest charges!

I'm now in the 83rd month of my three year loan . . . Six more payments and I own the hubcaps!

And everything is bargaining. There's no such thing as paying the list price. In fact there's only one way to get a new car these days. When the salesman says the list price is $4800—you say: "I'll take it!"—and when he drops dead, you steal the car!

CAR SAFETY

New cars have a tremendous safety factor—the price tag. It's so high you can't afford to buy one!

I know a fella who's making a fortune with an automobile safety device. He makes toupees for bald tires!

I just bought a new tire and I asked the salesman: "Is it safe?" He said: "Safe? This tire isn't made of rubber. It isn't even made of nylon. This tire is made of genuine apartment house leases!" I said: "Apartment house leases! Are they strong?" He said: "Did you ever know one you could break?"

And have you heard about the greatest safety device of them all? Costs $75 but it makes you feel completely secure. It's a big thumb that comes around like this: (HOLD YOUR RIGHT ARM OUT FROM YOUR SHOULDER WITH THUMB OUTSTRETCHED. IN A WIDE SWEEPING ARC, BRING YOUR THUMB AROUND AND INTO YOUR MOUTH—SUCKING IT AS A BABY WOULD.)

I bought a new car with defective brakes and I told the dealer: "I don't want you to stand behind this car—I want you to stand in front of it!

I won't say how I found out this car had defective brakes, but we no longer have to back out of our garage!

But in all fairness to the salesman, he didn't lie to me about the brakes. He said: "You'll love this car. There's no stopping it!"

Personally, I think they ought to be sporting about it. If they can't give you brakes that work—the least they could do is give you a louder horn!

This will go down in history as the Year of the Citrus. You've never seen so many lemons!

Detroit keeps calling cars back to correct defects. A funny thing happened to me on the way to the theater tonight—I got here!

Some cars are so dangerous it's no wonder they put alcohol in the radiator. I'd drink too!

For the first time we're finding out how dangerous cars are—even before the teen-agers get into them!

This morning I got a call from the outfit that sold me my car. They said I had a defective throttle. I said: "I get enough of that from my wife!"

CAR WARRANTY

What I like about buying a new car is all the guarantees you get. You're guaranteed for two years—or 24,000 miles—or until something goes wrong—whichever comes first!

I think every new car owner gets two shafts. One in the car and one in the warranty!

Be honest now. When was the last time you ever had anything go wrong with your car that was covered by the warranty? You bring in your car and right away they point out the Nudist Clause—All the things that aren't covered!

That's the reason they make these warranties so thick. So you can lean your checkbook against them when paying for repairs!

Lincoln said: "You can't fool all of the people all of the time." Obviously, Abe didn't know about warranties.

I have a great warranty on my car. The drive shaft is guaranteed for five years. Five years! It's the longest shaft in history!

CHARTER FLIGHTS

I just signed up for a wonderful charter flight to Europe. One hundred fifty dollars round trip. It features Seven Abreast Seating . . . six in the plane and one on the wing.

Believe me, it isn't bad sitting on the wing. If anything goes wrong with the engine you'll be the first to know!

And the wonderful part of this charter is they give you little extras. Like, with 289 people in the plane—one of the extras is taking off!

This could be the first plane in history with a hernia!

One charter flight was so crowded, the pilot went by boat!

The stewardess was a midget and she served coffee, tea, and condensed milk!

To organize a charter, you need a certain amount of people with a like interest. For instance, one charter consists of 75 people who couldn't get on any other charter!

Then there's another charter group that met while taking LSD. They're flying to Europe and they don't even have a plane!

CHILDREN

They say children keep a family together and that's right. Who can afford baby-sitters?

The ideal age for children is when they're too old for baby-sitters and too young to borrow the car.

Youth is that brief, golden period between training bras and surgical stockings.

Do you realize that ten-year-old kids are now wearing bras? And if that isn't bad enough, some of them aren't even girls!

It's amazing. You see kids wearing uplifts who don't even have ups!

Let's face it, the world is run by kids. Yesterday a Martian landed in Pasadena, walked up to a parent, and said: "Take me to your Little Leaguer!"

It isn't easy being a Boy Scout these days. Yesterday one of them helped three little old ladies across the street and two of them were hippies!

I'm for scouting. It teaches honesty, integrity, a dedication to truth, and all those qualities that make for solid citizens and lousy salesmen!

I like to dream the impossible dream. Like calling your kids in to dinner and having them come the first time!

Anyone who has ever eaten with four small kids knows why it's called din-din.

I got a wonderful way to cure kids who get lost in department stores and then you have to look for them. Don't!

I've got nothing against youngsters. I just make it a practice to follow the warning found on every bottle of medicine sold in the world today—KEEP AWAY FROM CHILDREN!

They say kids are disillusioned. You think kids are disillusioned? You oughta see their parents! One of them was looking at the Pill and saying: "Where were you in 1954 when I needed you?"

Nowadays kids are getting all of the things their parents never had when they were young—ulcers, neuroses, hypertension!

CHILDREN—EXPENSE23

Personally, I don't put down kids. Why, do you realize what this country would be like without kids? One million teachers would be working for the Post Office *full time!*

CHILDREN—CAMPS

Actually, we had no trouble sending our kids to camp this year. The TV set was broken.

It's one of those camps that are run strictly by the book. Your checkbook.

I just got the bill from that Indian summer camp my kids went to. I don't wanna say anything, but I think Custer got off easy!

Believe me, I know kids who go to a camp that's so exclusive— they have unlisted name tapes!

We have a five-year-old, and last summer even he went through an identity crisis . . . when he went to camp my wife sewed in the wrong name tapes!

That's the big difference between the generations. Nowadays a kid mopes around—they call it an identity crisis, and his parents spend five thousand dollars for a psychiatrist. Thirty years ago they spent 25¢ for a laxative!

CHILDREN—EXPENSE

They say teen-agers today have more than six hundred dollars a year to spend. I didn't believe it until Cadillac started making a skateboard!

Six hundred dollars a year! When I was a kid if I asked for 50¢ more a week, my parents thought I was keeping a woman!

But kids today spend. Did you know that kids buy half the soft

drinks sold in this country? That's why they have so many cavities—some of them even talk with an echo!

Nowadays if you have four kids, there's a new status symbol—
a sleep-in dentist!

I don't wanna complain about my kid, but last week he got five
cavities—in his braces alone!

Nowadays kids are so expensive, I finally figured out the answer
to that question: "What is a home without children?" Paid for!

CHILDREN—INTELLIGENCE

Kids today don't want to work. They want to lead the simple life.
And when you look at their report cards, you realize they're doing
it!

You keep hearing about dropouts. A dropout is a kid who goes to
the Fountain of Knowledge and just gargles a little.

You talk to kids and it goes in one ear and out the other. Which
isn't too surprising. There's nothing there to stop it!

I know a teen-ager who has a Polaroid span of attention. If he
can't get it done in sixty seconds, forget it!

Did you hear about the kid who was thrown out of high school?
They caught him selling the answers to the toothpaste test.

Nowadays a progressive teen-ager is one who drops out of high
school on Labor Day.

According to the latest statistics, the average American family now
has 2.7 children. And if you've talked to a teen-ager lately, you
know where the .7 comes from. A lot of them aren't all there!

I won't say he cheats on tests. Let's just say he always tries to sit behind round-shouldered honor students!

He's the type of kid who goes to school. Passes the toothpaste test and nothing else!

Remember the good old days when kids were seen and not heard? Now about the only time kids are seen and not heard is during oral quizzes.

I just figured out why Johnny can't read. Look at the headlines. Who'd want to?

Many teachers are concerned about the Seven Dwarfs Syndrome in their students. One out of seven is Dopey!

You gotta wonder about some of the students taking tests. It's incredible. One fella got his name wrong! What makes it so incredible—it was a multiple choice question!

I don't wanna say anything about my kids, but I go to P.T.A. meetings under an assumed name!

My kid showed me his first report card and at least he's imaginative. I asked him what "F" means and he said: "Fantastic!"

CHILDREN—PLAY

I guess you heard about the new game the kids are playing—ZIP CODE. It's like POST OFFICE only faster.

It's amazing how sophisticated children's stories have become. I just saw one where the good fairy is played by a hairdresser.

I'm a little shook up. I just heard three kids playing house. One was the mama; one was the papa; and one was the welfare investigator.

When you see them put something into their pockets, you gotta worry. Have you ever unloaded a six-year-old's pocket? It's like a woman's handbag with garter snakes. . . . My kid has so much in his pockets, we don't even worry about holes anymore—hernias!

I was always a rather timid child. You know how some kids sniff airplane glue? I licked library paste.

I had one of those progressive mothers. Like she had an ingenious little way to develop my creativity, my resourcefulness, my imagination. She put me outside and locked the door!

In my family, Creative Playthings were frogs, orange crates, and mud!

CHRISTMAS

Can you imagine if the Christmas story happened today? The Star of Bethlehem appears in the sky and the Air Force says it's a weather balloon!

I just figured out why we're having so much trouble in the world. All the wise men are under Christmas trees instead of in Washington!

I just met the most disappointed kid in the world. All he got for Christmas was his two front teeth.

I love to watch Dickens' *A Christmas Carol* on television. Scrooge is so mean, the opening scene shows him sending a size 40 bra to Twiggy.

Happiness at Christmas time is a bookie who takes gift certificates!

But what can be stranger than Christmas in the world today? Half the people are saying: "Peace on Earth!" And the rest are saying: "Where? Where?"

Can you imagine if the Christmas story happened today? The Three Wise Men would be fellas who got out of the stock market in time.

And nowadays the Three Wise Men wouldn't be riding camels. They'd jump in a cab and say: "Follow that star!"

When it comes to road maps, you can't beat following a star. Its simple, it's clear, and you don't have to refold it!

Even Confucius had something to say about this time of the year: "Man who get *Playboy* Calendar for Christmas really flip—pages!"

'Twas the night before Christmas and all through the house, not a creature was stirring. It was an A.A. meeting.

I'll tell you what I don't like about Christmas office parties. That looking for a new job afterward.

I know a kid who was born nine months after an office party. The boss named it "Oops!" 'cause it was a stenographic error.

I'm going to celebrate a traditional American Christmas. The tree comes from Canada; the ornaments come from Hong Kong; the lights come from Japan; and the idea comes from Bethlehem.

CHRISTMAS CARDS

Optimism is going into a shop on December 15th; ordering 250 imprinted Christmas cards; and saying: "I'll wait!"

Every Christmas I have this same terrible nightmare. That I buy 275 Christmas cards; address 275 Christmas cards; seal 275 Christmas cards; put stamps on 275 Christmas cards; take 275 Christmas cards down to the Post Office; push 275 Christmas cards through a slot —look up and read the sign over the slot: INCINERATOR.

Remember when: "Christmas! Bah! Humbug!" came from Scrooge? Now it's from mailmen!

CHRISTMAS DECORATIONS

Have you seen the decorations this year? I put on lavender ornaments; carmine tinsel; puce lights. I would have put on more but the tree threw up!

Things were so much simpler in the old days. They could do things like deck the halls with boughs of holly. I gotta get permission just to put up a calendar!

In the old days, they did wild things for Christmas. Like they brought home a yule log and it stayed lit for twelve days. Today, the only thing that stays lit for twelve days is my brother-in-law.

I just thought of the world's most unnecessary decoration—mistletoe in Peyton Place!

I have a wonderful landlord. Every Christmas he decks the halls with boughs of holly. It's cheaper than painting!

CHRISTMAS FOOD

For Christmas dinner, we always try to invite someone who's been beaten, downtrodden, ignored by the world. Like a Democrat.

Thanks to these holiday fruit cakes, people are suffering from a brand new stomach ailment—crushed ulcers!

A lot of these cakes come from Germany, and mark my words—Hitler is alive and mixing batter!

Someone just gave me a fruit cake, and I don't know if it's for Christmas or revenge!

You wanna go broke? Send one of these cakes airmail! . . . I think the ingredients are brandy, fruit, nuts, and cement!

The big advantage of fruit cakes is—they don't go moldy. 'Course, there's also a big disadvantage to fruit cakes—they don't go moldy.

Holiday fruit cakes are what you eat in April when your wife forgets to go shopping.

My butcher got real fancy this Christmas. He's selling smoked turkeys. I asked him: "How do you tell a smoked turkey?" He said: "By the nicotine stains on the wings!"

The way I see it—I've got nothing against smoked turkeys just so long as they don't inhale!

And Christmas is when they sell 80 million dollars worth of those gorgeous gourmet food packages. And inside, six bucks worth of food!

That's what you're paying for—cardboard, stuffing, and ribbons! Now I know what they mean by gift-rapped!

And the prices—$49.50, $69.50, $89.50. They're like CARE packages for J. Paul Getty!

This is the time of year when we all get bombarded with gift catalogues. Like if Christmas were canceled—Wisconsin is stuck with three million tons of cheese!

You look at these catalogues and they're loaded with fruit cakes and candies and seven-layer cakes and chocolate clusters. Just from turning the pages, my thumb gained seven pounds!

One outfit is selling chocolate-covered pickles for Christmas. Which is a great idea. Now you can have morning sickness before you get pregnant!

And everybody seems to specialize. One outfit sells nothing but cheese. Another has hams. Another has salamis. Another has chocolates. Then, in January, there's a company that really cleans up. Sells monogrammed Tums!

CHRISTMAS MUSIC

Frankly, I'm a little upset. I just heard someone singing "All I Want for Christmas Is My Two Front Teeth." It was my dentist.

I love the carol that goes: "'Tis the season to be jolly, tra-la-la-la-la, la-la-la-la!" I can never remember the words either!

You know what must be embarrassing? Singing "Come All Ye Faithful" in Peyton Place.

CHRISTMAS PRESENTS

For millions of Americans who have been saving their money for a rainy day—Christmas is the monsoon season!

I wanted to give my wife something she'd really enjoy for Christmas. Something that hasn't been available for a few years now. But how do you wrap up Frank Sinatra?

My wife has a peculiar sense of humor. She gave me a cordless shaver for Christmas. Sandpaper!

My wife still isn't talking to me from last Christmas. I asked her what she wanted for Christmas and she said: "Surprise me!" So at three o'clock in the morning I leaned over and went: "boo!"

One Christmas I gave my wife a $10 gift certificate and was she thrilled! She used it as a down payment on a $2000 coat!

It's kind of embarrassing, but my wife hasn't spoken to me since Christmas. I promised her anything—then gave her Arpège.

I don't wanna say anything about my wife but last year she gave me a pipe for Christmas. Unfortunately, there was a gas stove attached to it!

The year before that she gave me a butane lighter, and they're fun. For three days before we got it adjusted, the only thing I lit was the ceiling!

I gave my wife one of those mystery books for Christmas—a cookbook. With her, you can never tell how it's gonna come out!

I'm a little worried about the color-TV set my wife gave me for Christmas. It's a very unusual brand—Atwater-Kent!

I got one of those Christmas mail-order catalogues and I picked a deal where every month my wife gets something in the mail. It's called a Divorce!

Tell me. What do you do if you get a package marked DO NOT OPEN UNTIL CHRISTMAS—on December 26th?

I got a very unusual LP for Christmas: RAVI SHANKAR PLAYS IRVING BERLIN.

We've got an automatic elevator in our building and it's almost human. I didn't give it anything for Christmas, and this morning it let me off at the wrong floor!

CHRISTMAS—SANTA CLAUS

Christmas is a very fair season. There are kids who no longer believe in Santa Claus—and there are department store Santa Clauses who no longer believe in kids!

Believe me, it isn't easy being a department store Santa Claus. You spend eight hours lifting kids onto your lap and you'd swear the last one was wearing lead shorts!

In fact, December 26th is when department store Santa Clauses all over the country go out and have their laps resoled.

One kid looked up at Santa Claus and said: "Are you a politician?" Santa said: "Of course not. Why would you think I'm a politician?" The kid said: "'Cause you always promise more than you deliver!"

Let's face it. Santa Claus is no longer so unique. He wears this wild red outfit; he wears boots; he has a beard; and he only works one day a year. Do you realize how many teen-agers this fits?

But can you imagine how Santa Claus feels? Living in a whole world of takers and no givers?

I just had a crazy experience. A fella was complaining to me that he had to work on Christmas. It was Santa Claus!

If Christmas gets any more commercialized, they're going to be calling him Krass Kringle!

Show me a topless waitress who plays Santa Claus and I'll show you a nude Nick!

There's one advantage to living in New York City around Christmas time. If you can't afford presents, you can always tell the kids Santa Claus came through Central Park and got mugged!

September is when Santa Claus looks at all those dozens of elves in his workshop and says: "What do you mean you want more money?"

Santa Claus has his workshop at the North Pole. I've heard of being out of the high-rent district, but this is ridiculous!

CHRISTMAS TOYS

I gave my kid a bicycle for Christmas. Comes in 83 pieces and you have to put it together yourself. It's one of those gifts that keep on giving—ulcers!

I figure if I take two days off from work, I'll have it assembled by Easter!

Last Christmas I got one of those educational toys. Unfortunately, my wife found out about her.

I got my daughter one of those educational toys. It's a road race set that teaches her how to be a woman driver. When you change lanes, you don't signal!

And what about the prices on toys? Ten dollars, twenty dollars, thirty dollars! Nowadays, the problem isn't keeping up with the Joneses. It's keeping up with their kids!

Frankly, I could never understand why certain dolls are so popular. You know the ones I mean. They cry—from either end. . . . Costs you $6.98, and all you get for it is a kidney problem.

They have one doll that does nothing but cry. I think it got a look at its price tag!

Then there's a teen-age doll that's so realistic, it doesn't walk—it slouches.

I gave my kid a battery-operated tank, a battery-operated ray gun, and a battery-operated train set—and he loves them. All day long he sits around and makes towers out of the batteries!

One woman went up to a toy counter and said: "Do you have any electric trains for advanced children?" The clerk said: "What age do you consider advanced?" She said: "Forty-seven."

Toy soldiers are always popular and this year they have a brand new set. Chinese Nationalist Toy Soldiers. You never take them out of their box!

And there's a big group that wants to put a halt to war toys. It's called Taxpayers!

But kids seem to be fascinated by these war toys. I've got a baby—twelve months old—and already she's an expert on guided missiles —oatmeal!

CHRISTMAS TREES

Something's gotta be done about the price of Christmas trees. I bought one for $5.00, took it home, and my wife is wearing it as a corsage!

Skimpy? I told the guy who sold it to me: "It's amazing!" He said: "What's amazing?" "I didn't know Edsel made trees!"

We bought our tree two weeks ago and on Christmas morning, I'll never forget what I found under it—7000 needles!

You can't believe the prices they're getting for Christmas trees. They say only God can make a tree and sometimes I wish He would retail it too!

I paid $12 for a tree that welfare termites would have moved out of!

CITY PROBLEMS

(Name of city) is having a terrible problem with ladies of the evening. And if you're wondering why they're called ladies of the evening—have you ever seen one in the daylight?

I'd say you need only three things to appreciate these ladies—time, money, and myopia!

One of them was so old, I didn't know whether to call the cops or Social Security!

Frankly, I was a little embarrassed even to talk to her. Boy Scouts kept trying to help her across the street!

One girl has been in business so long, they've named a doorway after her!

I wouldn't call them streetwalkers. Let's just say they're Mercenaries in the Battle of the Sexes.

They're a different type of call girl. You don't call them, they call you. And if the answer is No, you oughta hear what they call you!

One girl came up to me and said: "You wanna have some fun?" So we went up to her apartment, and I finally found out what they keep in those big handbags—Monopoly!

Toy stores are even selling a Lady of the Evening Doll. You wind it up and it falls down—and it falls down and it falls down and it—

But these girls have made this town a much safer place. Now you can walk down the street, and the only ones yelling: "Help!" are chorus boys!

The way things are going, it won't be long before Sodom and Gomorrah will be considered model cities.

CHRISTOPHER COLUMBUS

In 1942 everybody thought the world was flat. And the way prices are going up, it soon may be!

I guess everybody knows the story of Columbus. What a trip! For three months they saw nothing but water. Then one day Columbus looked out at the horizon and saw trees! And if you think Columbus was happy to see trees, you should have seen his dog!

Can you imagine that first meeting between Columbus and the Indians? He's saying: "Chow!" and they're saying: "How!" . . . It must have sounded like the slow class at Berlitz!

Considering all that's happened in the last 474 years since Columbus landed, perhaps the Indians shouldn't have said: "How!" Maybe they should have said: "Why?"

COMPUTERS

They just invented a computer that's so human—on Monday mornings it comes in late!

Did you hear about the computer that drinks? They're calling it UNISWACKED!

I tell you, science is going too far. Now there's a computer that's so human, when it runs down they don't give it oil—they give it coffee!

But I really feel sorry for these machines—all alone in a hostile world. Nobody to program martinis into them when things go wrong.

They're never invited to the office Christmas Party.

I can just see an electronic brain sitting in a cocktail lounge, telling a well-stacked computer: "Nobody understands me!"

After a while they get bitter. I know one machine that only has one passion in life. Watching Westerns and rooting for the Indians!

And it flips over Frankenstein pictures. Keeps asking the monster: "What's a good-looking boy like you doing in a place like this?"

Frankly, I'm a little worried about my computer. It's that way over my battery-operated pepper mill.

Unfortunately, there's a religious difference. She's A.C. and he's D.C.

Believe me, I'm not prejudiced against automation. But I just want to ask you one question about computers. Would you want your daughter to marry one?

Is it true that in China, IBM cards are punched this way . . . (GESTURE A SLANT)?

CONSERVATION

Last summer a ranger at Yellowstone Park said his biggest problem was visitors feeding popcorn, candy bars, and marshmallows to the animals. Or—using his words: "Bear Pollution!"

I just want to know how the government explains the use of napalm to Smokey the Bear.

Scientists have just discovered why there are only forty whooping cranes left in the country. They used to be called whoopsing cranes!

I just figured out what they mean by the balance of nature. That's a girl who measures 40 inches wearing a bustle!

I'm getting a little worried. Lately the handwriting on the wall has been R.S.V.P.

CREDIBILITY GAP

You keep hearing about the Credibility Gap. That's a weather man saying: "Fair and warmer" while putting on an overcoat.

But there are all kinds of Credibility Gaps—like the Expos manager saying: "Men! We're gonna go out there and *win!*"

Before you get too critical of the Credibility Gap in things said and things done—consider your New Year's Resolutions.

CRIME

Thanks to the recent Supreme Court decisions, making an arrest these days is like cooking with Teflon. It's hard to make anything stick!

Crime in the streets is getting to be such a problem, yesterday I asked somebody for instructions on how to get to Riverside Drive. He said: "First you go to 79th Street. And if you make it—"

There's also a lot more violence directed at the police. Thirty years ago it was hard to find an unmarked cop's car. Nowadays it's hard to find an unmarked cop!

They say organized crime grosses 40 billion dollars a year and it's going higher. Never mind that. Is it going public?

Did you hear about the fourteen-year-old juvenile delinquent? He's too young to drive—so he steals only cars with chauffeurs.

Personally, I think we ought to take a more positive attitude toward parenthood. Like: IT'S BETTER TO BAIL OUT A JUVENILE DELINQUENT, THAN NEVER TO HAVE LOVED AT ALL!

This state is so romantic. They now have a special punishment for husbands who team up with their mistresses to get rid of their wives. It's an electric love seat.

I wonder if somewhere there's a gangster who's owned by a syndicate of singers?

I'm so unlucky, if I went walking down a dark, quiet street with my sword cane—I'd be mugged by D'Artagnan!

The most awful things are happening. Like I know a department store floorwalker who was mugged by a hippie—for his carnation!

Savoir-faire is a bank robber turning to the concealed TV camera and saying: "I'm a little late, folks, so good night!"

CUSTER

Custer is the fella who led 250 soldiers into 10,000 Indians. To this day, they're not sure if he was using a new tactic or the New Math!

I don't know where Custer got his military strategy from but, I think it was Egypt!

They claim that when Custer was down to his last six men, standing in a circle surrounded by 10,000 Indians—he made one of the great observations of military history: "All right! From now on, no more Mr. Nice Guy!"

Did you know that Custer had shoulder-length hair? Three times the Indians thought he raised the white flag, and it was only dandruff!

Six hundred thousand Indians called him Long Hair. Eight hundred thousand interior decorators called him Tiger!

D

DANCING

Did you ever get the feeling the frug is nothing but calisthenics with a beat?

It's like I was saying while doing the foxtrot the other day: "Dame Margot, you're leading again!"

The government is really getting tricky. Yesterday I took one of those dance courses where you just follow the footprints on the floor. Have you ever frugged into a draft board?

Maybe I'm old-fashioned, but I don't approve of belly dancers. Why can't they dance on floors like everybody else?

I won't say what some of these belly dancers look like, but I think Fatima is two words!

DANCING SCHOOLS

I really feel sorry for bachelors—never to know the sheer joy of attending a children's dance school recital. And it is a recital, 'cause they tell you about it for months in advance.

Terpsichore for tots is becoming a big business in America. I know three-year-olds who can do the time step. They can't walk—

I know a school that starts them so young, it offers a two-for-one special—classical ballet and toilet training!

Nowadays a deprived child is any kid who doesn't frug!

And if you don't send your little girl for ballet lessons, the P.T.A. puts you on report!

Confidentially, you shouldn't worry about the lessons. That a bank loan will take care of. It's the costumes. Paris Originals for midgets!

How can a yard and a half of gauze cost $42?

It's like this school never heard of plain pipe racks!

And the more scenes your kid is in, the more costumes she needs. You worry about having a second Pavlova. Who could afford it?

"Please, Zelda. Why can't you be like your friend Linda? A clod!"

Then comes the recital—2½ hours of "The Sugar Plum Fairy." I wouldn't want this much sugar if I had diabetes.

"The Sugar Plum Fairy" is the "When the Saints Go Marching In" of ballet schools.

I never had anything against the Russians until I was told one of them wrote this piece.

But it does teach the kids grace. Twelve years from now it's gonna be a pleasure watching them slash tires on tippy toes.

DEFINITIONS

A MOMENT OF TRUTH: what you have during bullfights and Washington press conferences.

ALCOHOLICS ANONYMOUS: an ad hic committee.

APPETIZERS: things you nibble on until you've lost your appetite.

BIRTH CONTROL: prenatal care.

BIRTH-CONTROL PILL: what a wife who wants children calls a husband who doesn't.

CAN OPENER: key to the washroom.

CONFIDENCE: what you start off with before you completely understand the situation.

CONSUMERS UNION: refrigerators!

CORRESPONDENT: A U-boat in the Sea of Matrimony!

DIPLOMATIC RELATIONS: I've never met any.

DIVORCEE: a wife whose option hasn't been picked up.

DON'T! That's the Ten Commandments by Speed-Reading!

DR. SPOCK: the Wizard of Ma's.

ECSTASY: when your conscience hurts and everything else feels good!

EDUCATED GUESS: what college students use to answer multiple-choice questions.

EYELIDS: windshield wipers for contact lenses.

Three fellas were sitting around trying to put a definition on the word "fame." One said: "Fame is being invited to the White House for a talk with The President." The second fella said: "No. Fame is being invited to the White House for a talk with The President —and when the Hot Line interrupts the conversation, He doesn't answer it." The third fella said: "You're both wrong. Fame is being invited to the White House for a talk with The President—and when the Hot Line rings, He does answer it, listens a moment, and then says: "Here, it's for you!"

FORTUNE COOKIE: a pizza with cramps.

FORTUNE TELLER: a bank employee in Texas.

FRUSTRATION: walking across a cribbage board in golf shoes.

GARDENING: a trowelmatic experience.

GROUP ADJUSTMENT: the whole family getting up to fix the color TV.

HAIR-RAISING EXPERIENCE: taking off a turtle-neck sweater.

HICCUP: a mini-burp!

HIPPIES: ragged individualists.

HONEST BARTENDER: one who makes a few bucks less than the boss.

INCOME TAX: the entry fee for the rat race.

INFLATION: mini-money.

JOINT CHIEFS OF STAFF: night-club owners.

MIDDLE AGE: that long period of time between I Don't Care and Medicare.

OLD MAID: a girl with a wait problem.

PACIFICATION PROGRAM: bringing your wife flowers after an argument.

A PACIFIST: someone who believes that fighting for what's right is a spectator sport.

PICKETING: the times that try men's soles.

POT LUCK: what you have in Haight-Ashbury if you don't get arrested.

RABBLE ROUSERS: pep pills for mobs.

REDUNDANCY: a sign saying MAKE LOVE, NOT WAR in Niagara Falls.

REFRIGERATOR: where you keep the leftovers before you throw them out.

RENO: where people go to kick the marriage habit!

SHOTGUN WEDDING: where you get married for better or hearse.

SOCIAL WORKER: a mother-in-law who's paid by the city.

SOCIALIZED MEDICINE: mouth-to-mouth resuscitation.

TACT: when you call an affair a mini-marriage!

TEEN-AGED: what happens to their parents!

TEEN-AGERS: people who work their fingers to the phone.

UP TIGHT: what happens when you take the Champagne Flight!

WEED KILLER: a pain in the crab grass.

DEMONSTRATIONS

These demonstrations are getting ridiculous. Do you know there are now six people picketing outside a prune juice company—with signs saying: HELL NO, WE CAN'T GO!

I just thought of a name for all these hippie demonstrations—The Crudesades!

What is with kids today? All they're interested in is social change, equal rights, human betterment! Tell me, where has sex failed us?

Remember the good old days, when teen-age protest was just a girl who said "no"?

Did you hear about the newest protest group? Wants to know why chicken soup isn't under Medicare?

Some college demonstrators spend so much time at sit-ins—when they go to class, it's a dumb-in!

Did you hear about the masochist who pickets police stations with a sign reading: PLEASE! BRUTALITY!

I think the instrument some of the demonstrators used to express their opinion, really says it. A bullhorn.

What can you really say about a person who pickets a Marine Recruiting office? He's rotten to the Corps!

I keep reading about student unrest. Maybe they just need a firmer mattress.

I finally figured out the semantics of it. A student activist is a juvenile delinquent with an I.D. card.

I know a college kid who's spent so much time picketing, he's a four-letter man—D-U-M-B!

All over the world, students are majoring in picketing, rioting, and trouble-making. Four years of college, and all they're learning to be is mother-in-laws!

What this country really needs is a mentholated beanie for hotheads!

But one college has come up with a fiendishly clever method of keeping a student's mouth shut. Peanut-butter malteds!

Demonstrators are people who live lives of riot desperation.

I know a parent who isn't taking any chances with his kid. He not only had his shoes bronzed, but his draft card too!

Whatever happened to the good old days—when the only thing that interested student bodies was student bodies?

The demonstrations all follow a pattern. The kids just plop down so that nobody can get through. It's a technique they learned ten years earlier in front of TV sets!

But in a way you have to admire these student demonstrators. They're the only ones I know who go limp and brag about it!

I don't know what students today are complaining about. Twenty-five years ago college kids had real problems—you ever try to swallow a dozen goldfish when at home you didn't even eat spinach?

Remember the good old days when civil disobedience was a puppy who couldn't make it to the curb?

I just wonder what these demonstrations will mean to future generations. Like, twenty years from now on the lawn in front of the county court house. Instead of a cannon, there's a scorched draft card!

I didn't realize how many hippies were involved until three groups sent in reinforcements: the Army, the police, and Five-Day Deodorant Pads!

I don't know who's teaching these kids democratic principles, but I think it's Attila!

A student demonstrator is someone who's so fed up with the mess the world is in, he wants to take over. And an adult sadist is someone who wants to let him.

A kid today wants his voice to be heard. And when it's changing, that isn't easy!

On one campus it was really a fight to the finish. The cops threw tear gas and the students retreated. Then the students threw hippies and the cops retreated!

And the cops were so free with their clubs, people have a new name for them—teeny-boppers!

Remember the good old days when a demonstrator was someone who sold you potato peelers?

DIETING

I know a woman who just went on a foolproof diet. You only eat when the news is good!

My wife is the eternal optimist. Claims she's gained ten pounds since the summer—but blames it all on a heavy cold.

I dunno. Either my wife goes on a diet or we're gonna have to let out the living room!

I'd like to explain why I'm a little overweight. It all started the day my rowing machine sank.

Desperation is a fella shaving before weighing himself on the bathroom scale.

I don't wanna brag about how much weight I've lost, but even my shoelaces don't fit!

When dieting, remember—what's on the table eventually becomes what's on the chair.

Have you noticed when you go on a diet, the first thing you lose is your temper?

A 900-calorie diet is when your stomach feels like Twiggy and looks like Gleason!

I just went on a fabulous new diet. It only calls for two things: 1, You eat only bagels and lox. And 2, You gotta live in Egypt!

I have an idea that could make me a fortune in the diet business. A kit that comes with 50 pills and a scale that lies!

The nice part about diet pills is—they really keep you going. Mostly to the diet doctor.

My wife went to one of these diet doctors and in two months, she lost $300!

And the pills they give you! I know a 200-pound lady who's spent more hours flying than T.W.A.!

Did you hear about the fat prospector who came staggering off the desert saying: "Metrecal! Metrecal!"

Dietetic foods are so expensive, you gotta lose weight. There's no money left over for cake!

Is it true they're going to put out a low-calorie popsicle called Metrecool?

When dieting, remember what a wise old Indian guru once said: "Banana splits make people double!"

I just came up with the perfect way to go on a diet. Five minutes before every meal—watch someone put their contact lenses in! . . . It's known as Instant . . . (PUFF YOUR CHEEKS)!

It's easy to lose weight. You don't need pills. You don't have to diet. You don't have to do without. All you have to do is when you get up in the morning go right into the bathroom, stand on the scale, and with your big toe, give that dial on the side a little nudge.

I just heard of a real humanitarian. Buys Metrecal wool for fat moths!

DISC JOCKEY LINES

To all you people listening to the show while driving to work—what makes you so sure you locked the front door?

I emceed a Golden Age dance and it was just wonderful. First time I ever heard (current far-out hit) played as a waltz!

I wish you people would start writing in about the show. I mean, how long will the sponsor believe we have an unlisted zip code?

I heard a record last week. It's the kind of a record you'd like to play with a laser needle!

At the sound of the chime, the time will be exactly (SOUND EFFECT OF CHIME). Sorry about that. After we bought the chime, we didn't have enough money left over to get a clock.

This is a 50,000-watt clear-channel station—and I'm mightly proud this channel is clear. Just shows you what can happen if you give up sweets!

Records now fall into three distinct categories: LOUD, LOUDER, and EH?

LEAD-IN TO COMMERCIAL: Did you ever have one of those mornings when you wake up—and your go-go has all gone-gone?

AFTER MONOTONOUS SIDE: That's a very interesting record. I think it's a dial tone with a beat!

Did you ever stop to think what an insecure job a deejay has? Your whole livelihood is based on people being too lazy to get up and flip the records themselves!

If you can call this a livelihood. I know a deejay whose bride left him 'cause he lied to her about what he was doing. He told her he was on welfare.

DIVORCE

I know a woman who got a divorce because of do-it-yourself. Every time she asked her husband to fix something, he said: "Do it yourself!"

In California, marriages break up so fast wedding photographers are using Polaroid cameras.

You follow all these big divorces—and you get the feeling it's not the principle of the thing—it's the money.

Women today don't want any problems. When they get married, it's a question of for richer or forget it!

So this fella is arrested for running away from his wife, but there's a difference of opinion on what he should be charged with. She claims it's desertion and he says it should be leaving the scene of an accident!

My wife better watch out. One more wrong move and I'm saying: "Turn in the HERS towel, kid—you're through!"

I tell you, I'd run away tomorrow if she'd ever show me how to pack a suitcase.

DOCTORS

Did you hear about the hippie baby doctor? He's sort of a slob-stetrician.

I know a fella who had a medical checkup and the doctor said he had to give up wine, sex, and song. The guy turned pale. He said:

"Doc, I can't! I'd starve to death!" The doctor said: "You'd starve to death by giving up wine, sex, and song? What do you do?" He said: "I sing dirty drinking songs!"

Sometimes I like to go off by myself and think deep, philosophical thoughts. Like—what are surgeons doing that they always have to wash their hands?

This surgeon is so rich he doesn't wash his hands. He dry cleans them!

Did you hear about the obstetrician who always asks for his patient's zip code? It's for faster deliveries.

A doctor is someone who acts like a humanitarian and charges like a TV repairman.

An apple a day keeps the doctor away. So does not paying your bills!

You haven't lived until you've gone to a medical convention. First time I ever saw pornographic X-rays.

Did you hear about the doctor who goes to burlesque shows? He's an eye, ear, nose, and throat man!

I just heard the saddest story. About a doctor who lost all his money on the horses—and in desperation he tried to rob a bank. But nobody could read his hold-up note.

A specialist is a doctor with a smaller practice but a bigger yacht.

Did you hear about the Irish throat doctor in Israel? His motto is: "Aaron, go 'Ah!'"

Picture what it must be like to be a family adviser. "Doctor, my husband has been unfaithful with the maid. He's been unfaithful with the baby-sitter. He's been unfaithful with the milkman." "With the milkman?" "It was a very foggy morning!"

DRAFT BOARD

You get a little worried about some of the fellas who show up at draft boards. Especially the ones who try to pronounce the eye charts!

I know a fella who's so unlucky, he opened a fortune cookie and found a draft notice!

Did you hear about the conscientious objector who studied karate? Broke a draft board in half with one chop!

Personally, I didn't burn my draft card. My wife burned it. She thought it was a steak!

And now they're talking about drafting women, which is ridiculous. Women in the Army have always caused confusion. I went up to one and said: "Sergeant Major?" And she said: "No, but he's trying!"

Some people are beginning to call their local draft board the Den of Inequity.

Maybe it's time we started to think positively. Like calling the Draft Board a Two Year Employment Agency!

You know what I find embarrassing about the draft board? Standing around nude with just a file folder in your hand. I don't wanna brag, but either they should give me clothes or a bigger file folder.

For you women who have never been to a draft board, it's where you walk around barefoot up to your chin!

Frankly, I was getting a little worried about that draft board. One time they asked me to take off all my clothes, and it was for the intelligence test!

You know what's embarrassing about the draft board? The way they tell you to take off all your clothes? I said: "Doc, tell me something. Are we gonna fight the enemy or tempt them to death?"

Remember when the draft board used to ask if you went out with girls? Now they just show you a *Playboy* Calendar. If you look at the dates—out!

Subtlety is a fella going to his draft board physical wearing a pair of slacks—that button down the side.

Yes. Show me the man who goes down to the draft board and takes off all his clothes except for a striped bow tie—and I'll show you a nude dude!

I didn't mind walking around in the nude so much. It was that doctor with the flower behind his ear!

And they have all kinds of strange tests at the draft board. Like, during one test I had to cough so much, they deferred me for bronchitis!

And they ask you such silly qestions, like: "If you were in command at the Alamo, what would you have done?" I said: "Fire the architect!" They said: "Fire the architect of the Alamo? Why?" I said: "No back door!"

And at every draft board they have the phonies. My favorite phony is the one—they put the blood-pressure test around his arm, start pumping it up, and he says: (IN PAIN) "Ooh!"

One of the major reasons men are rejected by the Army is flat feet. Do you realize how much trouble flat feet have caused in this world? I know a fella who got a divorce because of flat feet. His wife kept finding them in the wrong flat!

DRINKING

A bar is a place where you get dry martinis and wet change.

I don't wanna complain but somebody just stole the olive out of my cough medicine!

The trouble with going to those alcoholic meetings, you hear such awful things about what liquor can do to you that right away you need a drink to steady your nerves.

I don't want you to think this man is an ordinary, garden variety drunk. Far from it. Last year he donated his body to science, so he's preserving it in alcohol till they use it.

People who are driven to drink, rarely have trouble finding parking places.

You'd be surprised how much better the world looks if you see it through scotch-colored glasses!

I used to take a four-hour, five-martini lunch, but I had to give it up—for obvious reasons. It was cutting into my cocktail hour.

What a wonderful name for a store that sells hangover cures— a stupormarket!

Did you hear about the father who read that whiskey improves with age? So he bottled his teen-ager!

I don't drink to my wife. I drink because of her.

A sadist is someone who sends martini-flavored ice cream to A.A.

Alcoholics Anonymous. Doesn't it sound like a place where you can drink in secret?

They say there are four to five million alcoholics in this country. These, of course, are staggering figures!

I know a fish who swims like Dean Martin.

Incidentally, Dean Martin just finished a picture about the American Revolution, and it's very historical. Dean plays the bartender who pours the shot heard round the world!

Embarrassment is when you have a few martinis; go up to a svelte, stacked, swingin' chick at a party; suggest she go home with you—and she does 'cause it's your wife.

I just saw a crazy thing. A drunk standing in front of the Diamond Match Company singing: "Matchmaker, matchmaker, make me a match!"

He's sort of an alcoholic Don Quixote. He tilts even when there aren't windmills!

Did you hear about that new drink—vodka and prune juice? It's called a Hurry Mary.

It's one of those posh cocktail lounges where the two-cents plain is free—and the two-bit whiskey is a dollar and a half.

It's all right to drink, but who spends $500 a year just for coasters?

My wife's the sneaky type. Wants me to cut down on my drinking but won't say it. Just keeps putting larger olives in the martinis.

DRIVING

Parking lot attendants are the sixteen-year-old kids you pay 50¢ to drive the car you won't let your sixteen-year-old touch!

I saw one parking-lot attendant who's so young he still handles a car like a bike. Goes around corners on two wheels!

I said: "Would you go like that on a driver's test?" He said: "When I take one, I'll let you know!"

Parking lot attendants are great. These are the only fellas who can back up at 80 miles an hour. That's all they know how to do—back up! Mark my words, you rent a car and go to enough parking lots and Hertz will owe *you* money!

Guts is what you have when you double-park—alongside a police car.

One of the great pleasures of this life is coming up to your illegally parked car and not finding a ticket on it.

I just saw a scary thing. My wife teaching my mother-in-law how to drive.

I was just visiting a friend of mine in the hospital. He was teaching his wife how to drive when she suddenly turned right to let a bridge go by.

I'll never forget the time I gave my wife driving lessons. It was like being navigator to a kamikaze pilot.

Steering was the big problem. On our street you could have made a fortune selling Band-Aids to telephone poles.

And she never really parked the car—she abandoned it!

I won't say how far from the sidewalk she got, but who else has eight-foot curb feelers?

Did you hear about the wife who flunked her driving test—came home and said to her husband: "Well just don't stand there. Bray something!"

I'm a little worried. Either my wife has flunked her 65th driving test—or she's having an affair with the examiner!

I don't wanna say anything about the way my wife drives, but it's the first time I ever saw a warranty turn pale!

You know why they don't have Burma Shave signs on the Long Island Expressway? By the time you get to the second line—you've forgotten the first!

Remember when service station attendants used to give you the gas in the hose? Now you're lucky to get your tank cap back.

I just found out what happened to all those people who used to print the Ten Commandments on the head of a pin. They've all been hired by gas stations to put in that third number on signs advertising the price of gas.

Did you hear what happened to me on the freeway? A speed cop pulled me over. He said: "You were going 75 miles an hour!" I said: "Officer, I couldn't have been going 75 miles an hour. There's a governor on my engine." He said: "There's a governor on your engine? Prove it!" So I opened the hood and said: "Ronnie, tell him!" (adapt to your state)

The way people drive these days, I think a train whistles at crossings to keep up its courage.

DRUGS

A Broadway producer was on LSD and nobody knew it until he took an option on THE QUOTATIONS OF CHAIRMAN MAO TSE-TUNG —for a musical.

I just read about the nicest pusher in the world. Sells candy reefers to kids too young to smoke.

Hippies are very concerned about Southeast Asia—and anywhere else that grows poppies!

I'm fascinated by hippie neighborhoods. Like, where else can you see signs reading KEEP ON THE GRASS!

Personally, I always order my tranquilizer by its generic name—bourbon!

And now the latest thing is a combination birth control pill and LSD. It's for women who want to take a trip, but not to Dr. Spock!

Where else can you get hot dogs flavored with pot? That's right! Hot dogs flavored with pot! They're called Mariweenies!

If you really wanna drive your wife out of her mind, I've got just the thing: an aphrodisiac sleeping pill!

I'll have to work a little faster. I think my LSD is wearing off.

Have you heard about that LSD flavored toothpaste? You have 88 per cent more cavities, but who cares?

I know a teen-ager who's wasting his life on pot. He's crazy about fat girls!

Now there's a birth-control pill made of LSD. You fly so high, your husband can't reach you!

I didn't know my wife was on LSD until I said: "How about a week end in Las Vegas?" And she answered: "Great! Let's take the kids!"

Up in Berkeley they were having an LSD party and there was a knock on the door. Someone whispered: "It's the fuzz!" And the host said: "On Venus?"

Another two hippies were on LSD when a saturn rocket went by at 17,500 miles an hour! One of them turned to the other and said: "Man, I thought they'd never leave!"

Did you hear about the hippie who was so impressed with Lindbergh flying across the Atlantic—until he found out he did it in a plane?

You know who I feel sorry for? The middle-aged hippies. The ones who will go on a trip, but they wanna be back by eleven!

E

EASTER

Did you hear about the hen who sat on some of these candy Easter eggs? Hatched two chicks with a sugar problem!

If you don't think rabbits multiply, last Easter I gave my kids two chocolate bunnies. And the very next day they had 42 M & M's!

And they say: "Never pick up a rabbit by his ears." I don't know why they tell you that. It's the only part he isn't using!

ECONOMICS

I just figured out how to solve all of the economic problems of the country. We make another Disneyland out of Oklahoma and and use Texas for the parking lot!

Economists are afraid there will be another credit squeeze—and three old maids just changed their names to Credit!

What this country really needs is a completely new approach to our economic problems that has stood the test of time!

If you really want to shake up your wife, point out the fact that call girls are really the epitome of modern economic thought: Don't buy—lease!

I just figured out how to solve all of the economic problems of the country. Make complacency taxable.

EDUCATION

Have you looked at any of the back-to-school supplies they're selling? First time I ever saw a switchblade pencil sharpener.

If you don't think times have changed, when did you ever see a liquor store holding a BACK TO SCHOOL sale?

Personally, I'm against sex education in the schools. If you look at the statistics, what kids really need is a book on HOW NOT TO DO IT.

If kids mature any faster, it's going to be a race as to which they reach first—kindergarten or puberty!

When we graduated we felt the future was pregnant with possibilities. Nowadays kids have a different outlook. They feel the future is taking the Pill.

Some school boards are so childish. Like that one that fought for months to keep out a teacher with a long black beard—but they finally had to take her.

Progressive schools are where they never do anything to bruise a child's ego. One kid played hooky for three months, but they never called it that. They just said he flunked roll call!

Just for fun, I figured out my net worth using the New Math. It's $3,648,915. Under the Old Math, it's a buck and a half!

I don't wanna say anything about the New Math, but if you think calories don't count, you oughta see kids!

I've got a kid who thinks 2 and 2 make 6. He's got a wonderful future ahead of him—as a loan shark!

I dig this town 'cause it swings. We've got one school that's so progressive, for finger painting they use a nude model!

She's the type of college girl who, if she said she was awarded four letters, you'd be afraid to ask her what they were.

When I graduated I immediately put aside half of what I learned in college—'cause you can't make a living necking.

I can't say I was in the top half of my class—but I was in the group that made the top half possible.

Somebody suggested they might allow silent prayers in school. What do you think happens every time they pass out report cards?

My kid's a little afraid to go back to school this fall. He got the summer job his teacher was after.

Never pride yourself on knowledge. Remember, even a piece of lettuce knows one thing more than you do. It knows if that light really does go out when the refrigerator door is shut!

I asked my daughter what she learned in home economics class today and she said: "How to call Chicken Delight!"

Kids don't realize how important education is. Like one of them just got six months for stealing hubcaps. Not in jail—in a hospital. The car was still moving!

Hippies are against formal education. Like one of them just figured out by intuition what those things on the bottom of foreign movies are—words!

Remember when Abraham Lincoln used to walk twelve miles to school every day? My kid feels deprived if the bus doesn't pull in to the curb!

There's no question that education is a marvelous thing. I know a fella who went to college for six years and you oughta see him now. He's the only one who writes stick-up notes in Latin!

Did you hear about the professor who was such a lousy writer, he published and then perished?

I got an interesting circular in the mail this morning. It says: HELP FITE ILLITUHRASEE.

EGYPT

I just learned why the Arabs have stopped all archeological excavations. They found the world's oldest tomb; read the epitaph; and for the first time in history discovered that Adam and Eve had a last name—Schwartz!

Egypt is where one Pharaoh built a tomb that cost 20 million dollars! Just think—20 million dollars for a funeral. And that didn't include the organist!

Did you hear about the Egyptian general who went to a psychiatrist because of his delusions of grandeur? He wants to be an Israeli sergeant.

ELECTIONS

POLITICIAN "What did you think of my new campaign brochure?"
OCCUPANT: "I dunno. I'll have to ask my wastebasket."

Some people want to lower the voting age to eighteen, which is kind of frightening. The next President of the United States could have three major problems: Vietnam, inflation, and acne!

One candidate is making so many wrong moves they're calling him Mr. Blunderfull!

One candidate has even been compared to a carwash. He's automatically all wet!

A lot of third-party candidates will be offering the country a choice. A choice—isn't that what you get when you buy nuts?

Naturally, the incumbent always has a slight edge in these things. And if you don't believe it, ask Genghis Khan.

I have just one question for all the winning candidates: "What have you done for us so far?"

Sometimes I get the feeling the only reason they hold elections is to see which bumper stickers are right!

I've noticed one thing about bumper stickers. The ones who get them off the fastest are the losers!

I don't wanna complain, but on Election Day I was pretty badly hurt by the white backlash. The elastic broke in my jockey shorts!

It isn't easy for a woman to throw her hat into the ring. By the time people figure out what it is, the election is over!

Personally, I prefer off-year elections. You don't feel as guilty when you don't vote!

I wonder if (under-dog) ever gets the feeling he's overmatched? Like a surfer at Niagara Falls.

Talk about automation, (losing candidate) was just replaced by a voting machine.

I knew (losing candidate) was in trouble when he came on television looking green. And we don't have a color set!

Nobody knows what the election in (state) means, but the new state flower is hemlock.

It was a fantastic election. Eighty million Americans took time off from work to vote—and 50 million of them did.

EMCEE LINES

NO BUSINESS: This looks like the birth-control clinic at Sun City.

I wanna dedicate this song to Francis Scott Key—the only man ever to learn all the words to "The Star Spangled Banner."

We will now call on our instant-replay camera so you can get a close-up of that joke dying!

I'd like to sing some old-time, sentimental favorites—but please, no crying in your drinks. They're watered enough as it is.

Personally, I think the management overdoes it a little. Like, I don't mind their watering the liquor. You gotta expect that in a night club. But the ginger ale?

I won't say the drinks are watered, but we've got the only whiskey in town that's fluoridated!

In fact, next week they may cut out liquor altogether. Just go with club soda and bourbon-flavored stirrers!

Statistics show that more accidents occur at home than anywhere else. So drink up! What do you wanna go back there for?

We've had wonderful audiences in here on Thursdays, Fridays, Saturdays, and Sundays. It's only the rest of the week I feel I should have become a butcher.

I don't say this to get your sympathy—but I come from a broken home. You see, we own a Great Dane!

We have a new vocalist who's got three numbers I know you're gonna be wild about—39-25-36.

I think she did a magnificent job in spite of a very trying day. The owner tried. The lifeguard tried. The bellboy tried.

Have you noticed the size of the portions they serve in here? I won't say they're small, but you people may be eating the world's first frozen transistor dinners.

Be honest now. What do you think of our chef? Really—what this man doesn't know about cooking you could put in a stomach pump!

We had an Englishman in here last night. I could tell he was English. He was eating alphabet soup and dropping his H's.

EMPLOYMENT

I guess you heard about that new office machine that does the work of three women. Goes to the washroom 26 times; makes 48 personal phone calls; and takes up a collection.

You know what I resent? All these office collections for babies. So the receptionist on the fifth floor goofs. I gotta pay for it?

Remember when it was vitamin pills that gave you the Daily Minimum Requirement? Now it's workers.

I've got nothing against four-hour lunches—but it sure louses up the afternoon coffee break.

They're never gonna get me to accept a four-day week. That's just a sneaky way to beat me out of two coffee breaks!

According to the latest statistics, there are 3 million Americans who aren't working. And there are even more, if you count those with jobs!

Last week 837 people left their jobs. Five quit and the rest told the boss about his breath.

Now there's a new mouthwash that's flavored like bad breath. It's for people who want to go on unemployment insurance!

I can remember when Social Security was Sen-Sen.

Everybody's talking about take-home pay. You know why you have to take it home? It's too little to go by itself!

ENGLAND

Everything's put so nicely in England. A call girl is known as a maid-to-order.

The British are doing such great things in the Arts, sometimes I wish Paul Revere had minded his own business!

I just had an interesting thought. If King George III were alive today, I wonder if he'd want us back?

In Swinging London, you can tell the people are determined to do their utmost to restore the prestige and power of Britain. They're betting much faster!

I just found out why they say London swings. There's this terrible girdle shortage!

And if you're planning to try British food, may I make a suggestion? They have these battery-operated stomach pumps—

But I don't blame the British for the way they cook. Do you realize if it wasn't for heartburn, these people would never get warm?

The British still like their drinks warm. I was in London for three weeks and there's only one thing you can count on getting cold—and that's hot water.

Don't you think Britain was a lot better off when George Arliss was running it?

You remember Great Britain. A number of islands entirely surrounded by hot water!

EYEGLASSES

So many people are wearing glasses, if you've got perfect eyesight, they call it prescription eyeballs.

I'm so nearsighted, I need contact lenses just to see my glasses!

I won't say how long I've been paying for them, but I call them contract lenses.

F

FADS

This year, the newest thing in women's hairdos is men!

Three hundred years ago Lady Godiva rode through the streets naked except for her long flowing hair. Today it'd be Lord Godiva!

Teen-agers have a new fad now—covering things with toilet paper. It's like a lot of people have been saying all along—they don't know it from a hole in the ground!

In Michigan, they covered a house with 3000 feet of toilet paper. They would have covered it with 4000 feet only that would have been silly!

It's fascinating. You see these kids walking along with six rolls of paper in their hands and three in their pockets. They look like a tourist in Europe!

And if you think adults are discouraged by all this, what about trees? One redwood watched a teen-ager throwing around toilet paper, nudged the pine tree next to him and said: "Look! Look what Sam gave his life for!"

FALL

And so, as we head into the fall, let's all remember the Beach Goer's Motto: Old suntans never die; they just fade away!

Autumn is that period of the year when the days are getting shorter and the shorts are getting longer.

And the schoolteachers—they have a little poem dedicated to September:

> The saddest words of tongue or pen;
> Here come all those kids again!

Here it is autumn. The leaves are turning amber. There's a golden hue to the land. And just as we're beginning to regain a little of our faith in the world—another TV season begins.

I'm not criticizing the intellectual level of TV programing, but one new show won't have a laugh track. It'll have a Duhhh Track!

All the stations are showing little hot flashes of what the new shows will be like. In fact, this season looks to be the menopause of the industry!

I won't say what the new TV shows are like, but if the fella next door uses his home diathermy, you're glad!

And this year it's amazing how many movies will be shown on TV for the first time. Plus a lot I'd like to see shown for the last time.

I can remember when they said television would kill the movies. Now it's more like a mutual suicide pact.

If the new comedy shows are representative of what's to come, ten years from now there's gonna be a tremendous shortage of laugh tracks.

And if there's anything to the Pavlovian Theory of Conditioned Response—every time we hear a laugh track, we should yawn!

FARMING

I tell you, it's going too far. I know a fella who gets paid $8000 a year not to plant things—and he's an undertaker!

Do you know they're injecting female hormones into beef cattle? Neither did I until I saw this Texan go into a steak house like this (BOW-LEGGED) and come out like this (MINCING)!

I know a dairy farmer who's so tired of his job, he won't even go to a topless night club.

Say, I just found out where all that chemical fertilizer comes from. Plastic horses!

FLU

I'm so unlucky. Last week I got a cold, so I took that stuff that opens the nasal passages. And while they were open, I caught another cold!

I had a cold last week, and it was something! My nose did more running than a tourist in Mexico!

I've had so many penicillin shots, I look like a junkie with a terrible aim!

I'll tell you how many penicillin shots I got. I sent my red flannels to the tailor. Had the flap taken out and a bull's-eye put in!

And flu shots are so expensive—what this country really needs is pennycillin.

Say, wouldn't that be a wonderful name for a nurse who gives flu shots? Fanny Hill?

My doctor is really up on these things. He was telling me about a politician in Washington who's got the Kleptomania Virus. I said: "The Kleptomania Virus? Is it catching?" He said: "No. It's taking!"

Incidentally, the government is finally going to do something about this flu epidemic. Starting Monday, it's illegal to exhale!

Did you hear about this family in Wisconsin who all have terrible coughs? They're known as the Green Bay Hackers!

But I know one fella who got quick, quick relief from cold misery. A divorce!

FLYING SAUCERS

I know a fella who calls his wife a UFO—a Usually Friendly Object.

Every spring hundreds of people see flying saucers. And I drink a little myself.

People claimed they saw this long metallic object with flashing lights at either end. Maybe it was two police cars necking!

Personally, I'm very cynical. One time a flying saucer landed right on my front lawn. A little green man got out and said: "You wanna fly to Mars?" I said: "What's the movie?"

And I just figured out why these flying saucers don't stay too long. Maybe it's a seven-planet tour in fourteen days!

Now they say those flying saucers are caused by gas. I didn't even know my wife cooked for them!

If flying saucers are really swamp gas, can you imagine what this is gonna do to science-fiction movies? I mean, how will it look— the Air Force fighting back with bicarbonate?

FOLK SINGERS

Isn't it amazing the way folk singers are specializing? Now there's a group that sings Freedom Songs in Leavenworth!

I can't believe that some of these folk-rock groups can play the electric guitar that bad. I keep thinking it must be something else —like the electricity is flat!

Now there's a folk singer who plays an Early American Electric Guitar. It comes with a kite and a key!

And folk singers are getting younger all the time. I know one folk singer who's so young, the only trouble she's got to sing about is diaper rash!

It finally happened. As of six o'clock last Tuesday, there were 1.6 billion folk singers in this world—and 1.5 billion folk!

FOOD

A biologist claims there will be a world-wide famine by 1975. A world-wide famine by 1975! And the only ones who'll be ready for it are Jack E. Leonard and Kate Smith!

A world-wide famine by 1975! I got news. Go into any restaurant, order a $2.00 steak and you'll think it's already begun!

Personally, I won't believe there's a famine until I open the center fold of *Playboy* and it's Twiggy!

Nobody will ever starve in America just so long as there's a Welcome Wagon and you can move every day!

You know what's a great combination? Pepsi and oysters! It's for people who think young and feel old.

I've been eating that breakfast cereal that's great for children, and it really is. My wife is pregnant!

I'm fascinated by all the different kinds of breakfast cereals. One box is for kids who want to be baseball players. Another box is for kids who want to be astronauts. They even have a box for kids who want to be Twiggy. It's empty!

Show me a fella who eats nothing but pastrami, bagels, lox, and pickles—and I'll show you a man with a deli belly!

Did you hear about the fish market that sells sole food?

Remember when you could only buy milk by the quart? Now it comes in the gallon, two quart, quart, pint, and Mickey Rooney sizes. The Mickey Rooney size—that's a half pint!

Guts is putting on a new shirt to eat an egg-salad sandwich.

Say, wouldn't it be embarrassing if somebody won the Pillsbury Bake-Off with a Betty Crocker recipe?

It's a proven fact that coffee does stimulate you. You might say it's the poor man's LSD.

I just saw a crazy bumper sticker: JULIA CHILD EATS AT CHICKEN DELIGHT!

FOOD PACKAGING

I got an idea how breakfast food companies sell 20 per cent more corn flakes than they're selling right now—fill the boxes!

More and more, wide-open spaces have nothing to do with Texas—but cereal boxes.

Some of them are packed so loose, I don't know if I'm buying corn flakes or square maracas!

And the instructions are priceless. SERVES FOUR—if it's Lent and you're fasting.

Have you ever speculated on what these FOUR look like? 98 pounds. Not each—together! . . . Stomachs rumbling, hollow cheeks, the only Americans getting CARE packages!

I'll tell you another gripe I've got with the food companies—sizes. Nowadays every package comes in four distinct sizes: LARGE, SUPER-LARGE, GIGANTIC, and ENOUGH.

When was the last time you found anything labeled SMALL? There's no such thing as SMALL anymore. SMALL is now COMPACT LARGE!

And you can't go by appearances. One counter has three different boxes. Like this (INDICATE WITH YOUR HANDS A BIG, TALL, SQUARE BOX), like this (A HUGE ROUND BOX), and like this (A GIGANTIC WIDE BOX). And they all hold the very same thing—three ounces of potato chips!

You just gotta be impressed by the potato-chip makers. Anyone who can get 79¢ for one potato and an acre of cellophane deserves respect!

FOURTH OF JULY

The July 4th week end is really a fabulous experience. It gives you the opportunity to spend hours sitting on hot, crowded highways—so you can spend hours sitting on hot, crowded beaches!

You know the nice thing about the 4th of July nowadays? You don't hear firecrackers anymore. The kids used them all up in June!

July 4th is kind of an interesting holiday. Like, try explaining to your kid why he can't buy firecrackers but the government can buy H-Bombs.

FRANCE

The Marquis de Sade was a French nobleman who got his kicks from making people miserable. We have the same thing today, only they're called wives.

I've been boycotting French products and believe me, that isn't easy. Have you ever seen Eskimo postcards?

It's a comforting thing about those beaches on the Riviera. The sun is so strong, you can't tell if people are burning or blushing.

Have you ever eaten in a Paris restaurant? The real waiters are the customers!

It's kinda hard to describe a French waiter. Picture a New York cab driver with an apron!

I never have any trouble in French hotels. The first thing I do is rap on the counter and say: "*Je parle Berlitz!*"

You know what I like about France? Where else can you complain to your wife that your girl friend doesn't understand you?

To give you an idea what kind of a swingin' country this is— their third largest industry is back-dated marriage licenses!

You gotta admit travel agencies have a sense of humor. Calling anything that takes you to Paris a "thrift season."

G

GAMBLING

Las Vegas is where the sight-seeing bus never leaves the hotel. It couldn't top it!

This is Irish Sweepstakes time again—sometimes known as Las Vegas with a brogue.

And the day after they announce the winners, Internal Revenue is singing: "Did your money come from Ireland?"

But inflation has really changed things. It used to be, you won $75,000 and you quit your job. Now you check to see if it'll affect your welfare payments!

I love to gamble. Last week alone I went to every filling station in town and bought 342 gallons of gas—just to enter 55 different contests. Sometimes I wish I had a car!

GARDENING

I love to experiment with flowers. Like last year I crossed a rambling rose with a pansy. Now the rose still rambles, but it takes very small steps.

I just bought a rather unusual tree. Twenty feet high. It's a Bonsai Sequoia.

The trouble with having a green thumb—it's often accompanied by a red face and purple knees.

It kinda shakes your faith in people—like finding out Thoreau had a gardener.

Did you hear about the soft-hearted gardener? He built a special nursery for unmarried mums!

I didn't do much over the week end. Just read some science fiction —the new seed catalogues.

Isn't it sweet of these people to worry about my garden—and I can't even see it under the snow?

I think these seed catalogues are really the triumph of hope over experience. For the last five years, I haven't so much grown flowers as buried seeds.

But each March the seed catalogues come in and you get carried away with ambition, enthusiasm, and peat moss!

It's the pictures that really do it. These magnificent four-color reproductions of roses, chrysanthemums, marigolds. And the very first sign of the mature, knowledgeable gardener, is the realization that whatever he does, whatever he buys, whatever he grows will look nothing like these pictures!

Personally, I think they're all posed by professional flowers at $50 an hour.

Some of the captions under the pictures get pretty exotic. One year they were describing a particular type of violet and they said: "Not much in beds but grows wild in the woods!" . . . I didn't know if I was reading *Burpee* or *Playboy!*

And they're always cross-pollinating and changing and improving the flowers—as if God needed help.

The big triumph this year is an odorless, thornless rose that lasts for months. I saw one and it's really remarkable. You can't tell it from plastic!

But the seeds, bulbs, and plants are really the smallest part of gardening. The biggest part is blisters. . . . You spend ten hours on a Saturday planting tulips—and your knees are gonna look like they're blowing bubble gum!

Gardening brings almost as many people to their knees as religion —only the words they use are a little different.

The government wants to get people fit? All it's gotta do is send every American a packet of mixed seeds with a note: "Dig this!" After one summer, they'll either be fit or throw them!

GERMANY

Did you hear about the traffic signs they have by the Berlin Wall? One says: YOU ARE NOW LEAVING EAST GERMANY. THAT'S WHAT YOU THINK!

Sometimes I get the feeling that all Germany has done is beat its swords into .45-caliber plowshares!

Germany is starting a world-wide peace campaign and it's kind of interesting the way they announced it. They said: "We're going to work for peace. And anyone who stands in our way, will be crushed!"

Wouldn't that be a frightening thought? A German call girl? It sounds so ominous. Like when she calls, you listen!

GOLD

A balance of payments problem comes about when you have two opposing but unequal quantities—like, one salary and one wife!

They say Europeans are trying to get rid of American dollars, but I notice none of them are holding 1¢ sales.

Europe is getting obsessed with gold. I know a tourist who was mugged for his fillings!

Nerve is when an undeveloped country we're giving aid to—asks for it in gold.

For years gold has been leaving the country, but now it's beginning to run charters!

You wanna know how much gold has left the country? The government just started renting out rooms—in Fort Knox!

Frankly, I'm worried about all this gold leaving the country. Like, who's in command at Fort Knox—Custer?

I figure that in another ten years, Fort Knox will make Mother Hubbard's cupboard look crowded.

Sometimes I think our only hope for solving the balance of payments problem—is to put Fort Knox in a Xerox machine!

GOVERNMENT SPENDING

I didn't realize how hung the government was for money until Internal Revenue started selling gift certificates.

My wife and the government have the same problem. They both like to do a lot of things they can't afford!

I just figured out what we've been doing wrong. We've been giving Metrecal to people when it's the federal budget that needs it!

Fortunately, we won't have the National Debt to worry about any more. Howard Hughes just bought it.

He who builds a better mousetrap will soon find the government voting $85,000 to build a better mouse!

People who think the world owes them a living, now have a government that agrees with them.

Giveaway programs could be creating a whole new social class—the down and in!

Personally, I've got nothing against the government wanting to fight poverty. It's just that they always want to use my savings as ammunition!

Have you noticed, as Congress gets to the end of each session, they start passing billion-dollar spending bills like it was nothing? I think they suffer from boodle fatigue!

I won't say where all the money we send to Washington is going, but they just sent out for six more drains!

The latest statistics show that 4 million Americans are idle. Unfortunately, most of them work for the government!

Remember the good old days when a government handout was a politician offering to shake?

GRAMMAR SCHOOL

But you know why I like to send my four year old to day school? It's the only time a kid gets to see a teacher. As soon as they start in grammar school, the teaching machines take over. I know one kid who's been going to public school five years—and the only warmth he ever gets in a classroom is when he stands near the bulb in the projector!

Can you imagine how difficult it is for a kid to identify with a Bell and Howell? . . . At the end of the term you don't bring it a handkerchief—lens cleaner!

Not that teaching machines are anything new. I can remember an English teacher who used to come in pretty well oiled when I was a kid. . . . Only instructor who ever taught Bacon fried.

Have you ever noticed second- and third-graders going to school in the morning? They're all lopsided. And it's not because of malnutrition—books! You see them staggering down the street with a briefcase, thirty pounds of books, and a fan letter from Charles Atlas!

You wanna know what to put under their pillows when they get promoted? It's simple—a hernia belt!

I've got a seven-year-old daughter who's already a perfect 36—around the biceps!

Remember when we went to school, the heaviest thing we had to carry was a lunch box? Remember those lunch boxes? Tin attaché cases for peanut-butter sandwiches!

My teachers always thought I was a quiet kid. What quiet? With all that peanut butter, I couldn't open my mouth!

Frankly, you couldn't really call it peanut butter. Epoxy Glue with calories!

And no lunch box would be complete without a half-pint thermos bottle—which you broke the first day.

I think most kids learn about lying because of that thermos bottle. Your mother said if you ever broke it, you'd never get another one. And she's out buying them in the handy six-pak!

But who can ever forget the taste of fresh fruit—after spending a morning in that hot, overcrowded, unventilated lunch box? If you had a banana, you didn't eat it—you drank it!

And apples. I thought brown was their natural color!

You're always hearing about a good hot lunch? For me this meant grapes!

I'm all shook up—ever since I read about that grammar school the cops raided. The one with the marijuana jelly beans!

H

HALLOWEEN

This time of year the holidays come so close together, I don't blame kids for getting confused. Like, yesterday I saw a kid light a candle inside a turkey and yell: "Merry Christmas!"

I don't wanna say anything about a restaurant I go to, but on Halloween, kids tip over the kitchen!

I'm getting a little suspicious of my wife. For Halloween she didn't put apples in a tub of water—piranha!

I love Halloween. It's the only night of the year when Phyllis Diller looks right!

HIPPIES

You wanna know what kind of a crazy mixed-up world we're living in? A hippie just mugged another hippie for his love beads!

Did you hear about the hippie parents who heard their kid say a clean word—so they washed out his mouth with dirt?

Sometimes I wonder if the hippies aren't winning. I just saw a Rolls-Royce with a flower decal.

Twenty years ago, only senile old men wore beards. Now it's senile young men!

Perhaps this will clarify matters. When a hippie says of our society: "I just can't see it." That isn't his philosophy. It's his haircut!

It's kinda hard to describe the average hippie's haircut. Picture a haystack in heat!

Did you hear about the girl who went to a love-in and nine months later was in a psychedelicate way?

It's kinda hard to describe the people at these love-ins. It's like they emptied all of the 42nd Street movie houses into a park!

I know a hippie who keeps stealing his mother's beads. At least she hopes he's a hippie!

I know a fella who's against those barefoot hippies in his own quiet way. He just bought three dogs.

Have you noticed how cool and relaxed and mellow I've been the last few months? It's all because I'm keeping up with the Joneses —and they're hippies!

HIPPIES—CLEANLINESS

I know a hippie who refuses to be brainwashed—and it doesn't stop there!

"What do you give to the hippie who has everything?"
"D.D.T.?"

Don't ever call a hippie a slob. For some of them, that's a step up!

They call hippies the flower children, and the way some of them smell, I think they're using a little too much fertilizer!

I know a hippie who's a hygienic atheist. He doesn't believe in baths!

Did you hear about the hippie kid who was bad? So his hippie parents made him stand in the corner—of a shower!

Thanks to a certain pungency, hippies have added a brand new expression to the language. It used to be: "Hip. Hip. Hooray!" Now it's: "Hippie. Hippie. Hoo Boy!"

You know the nice thing about being a hippie? If you want to lose five pounds, all you have to do is take a bath.

Hippies march to the beat of a far off drummer. And if you've ever smelled one of them, you know why he's far off!

You know why a hippie will never be heavyweight champion of the world? They all fight dirty!

Hippies are people who dress alike, talk alike, smell alike—and what are they against? Conformity!

HISTORY

The scene is a clearing in the heart of darkest Africa. Two men stand in the middle of it:
"Dr. Livingstone, I presume?"
"That is correct, Mr. Stanley."
"Doc, I got this terrible pain in my back." . . .
"Why tell me? I'm a dentist!"

The twenties were kind of an interesting period. Nowadays, adults are always talking about a dialogue with teen-agers. In those days it was a monologue: "Shut up!"

In the twenties, if you wanted beer you brought your own pail to the corner saloon. If you wanted milk, you brought your own pail to the corner grocer. Same pail. I was the only two-year-old on the block in Alcoholics Anonymous!

Not that it helped. It isn't easy to get a two-year-old to go dry.

Remember the old movies? They were completely silent except for the piano and kids walking around in corduroy knickers.

In the twenties, you could buy a car for $600. Nowadays, that's a down payment on the insurance!

Betsy Ross was the woman who sewed the first American flag for George Washington. George looked down at the 7 red stripes, the 6 white stripes, the 13 stars, the field of blue—and uttered those historic words: "Betsy sweety—wouldn't you say it's a little busy?"

I just saw the most realistic historical restoration ever. The four-poster bed is unmade and George Washington's clothes are hanging over a chair.

I just figured out why it's called the extinct dinosaur. Who could make a deodorant that big?

Remember the good old days—when a hooker was just a one fingered pickpocket?

I don't mind history repeating itself, but lately it's been eating radishes!

HOLIDAYS

February 22nd: As you know, George Washington was the Father of our Country—and King George III was trying to be the Pill.

Did you know that George Washington wore false teeth made of wood? That's right—made of wood! When he took the toothpaste test he had 21 per cent fewer knotholes!

I had the swingin'est holiday ever and it was all so simple. I just bought my secretary a $5.00 piece of jewelry; added two zeros to the price tag; and forgot to take it off!

I just love spending the Labor Day Week end in New York. Just think—three whole days of parking spaces!

Have you ever noticed—most holidays are a day off followed by an off day?

HOLLYWOOD

In Hollywood, girls never live in sin. They just have unlisted husbands.

I wanna give you an idea what kind of a swingin' town this is. Have you ever played Strip Monopoly?

I didn't know how wild this town was until I went into a strip club and heard three fellas yelling: "Take it off! Take it off!" And this was to the bartender!

Hollywood is where the kids don't play Good Guys and Bad Guys. They play Clients and Agents.

They say George Washington never told a lie. He never would have made it as an agent!

And the Hollywood schools are fantastic. This is the only town where truant officers work from a surfboard!

Hollywood report cards are interesting. They're 4 inches wide and 15 inches long—so all of the parents can sign them.

Did you hear about the elephant who appeared in so many jungle pictures, he went Hollywood? Just had his tusks capped!

HOLLYWOOD VERSION: a neurotic is a low-budget psychotic.

In Hollywood, an intellectual is anyone who reads Freeway signs without moving his lips.

If you don't think Hollywood is fascinating—where else can you see people playing strip poker for money, just to make it interesting? . . . It's called PAY AS YOU SHOW.

In Hollywood there's only one minority group—the solvent!

HORROR MOVIES

You know what puzzles me about the Frankenstein movies? The way the monster always walks around with his arms outstretched. I haven't seen anybody walk like that since my wife fell asleep under a sun lamp!

Haven't you ever wanted to talk to the monster like a Dutch uncle? "Frankie, baby. . . . There's nothing personal in this but—where did you get that coat? . . . You, it isn't! . . . And that walk, sweety. Chiropodists aren't that expensive!"

Actually, the Frankenstein monster has a very deep psychological problem. He thinks people are staring at him.

They wanted to put him in analysis, but the way he moves it would have taken 45 minutes just to get to the couch!

I can see the psychiatrist now: "Before we begin, let me say that dreams, nightmares, horrors, the screaming meemies, are very important—and fella, you're really giving 'em to me!"

Fortunately, they recognize the problem, and in the very next picture Dr. Frankenstein is planning to mate the monster. Now they gotta figure out to what?

Let's face it. He's thirty-three years old and the only charge he's ever gotten is from electricity. . . . This could do things to a fella. For three years he was that way about Hoover Dam!

We don't hear too much about Dracula any more 'cause he's suffering from a very embarrassing condition. Especially for a vampire. It's called—loose dentures! . . . Yes, thanks to upper-plate wobble, Dracula now has three major worries: A cross, a stake through the heart, and a tough throat!

I just saw a great horror picture. This monster, 2000 feet high, eats Mexico City! And the very next day, he drinks the Kaopectate factory!

I just saw a modernized version of *King Kong*. You know that big scene where King Kong picks up the girl? In this version, she doesn't even scream. What for? She's taken the Pill.

Did you know they tried to make one of those monster pictures down in Alabama? But every time King Kong walked down the street, somebody said: "Mornin', Sheriff!"

Hollywood just turned out its first hippie horror picture. Six hippies are driving along a lonely country road when suddenly they're confronted by an alien presence—Dial Soap!

HOUSES

If you want to know precisely where your own property ends and your neighbor's begins—watch him carefully the next time he cuts the grass.

I don't wanna wish anything bad for Egypt, but the fella who built my house should have built their pyramids!

I don't know why they say new houses don't have enough closet space. They have plenty of closets. It's just that builders have a different name for them—guest bedrooms!

I don't know why they call them "family rooms." All you ever see in them is a TV set and the neighbors' kids.

It's amazing what they're doing to bathrooms these days. I saw one that's so modern it's got a bucket seat!

HUMAN RELATIONS

You don't know what it is, living with a wife and a mother-in-law. It's like a weak martini—2 to 1.

I haven't been so disappointed since a starlet invited me up to her apartment to look at her etchings—and we looked at her etchings.

Did you ever feel really foolish? Like bringing candy to the host of an orgy?

The saddest story I ever heard, was about an unmarried girl who's expecting. So she goes to another city leaving a false forwarding address; registers in a small hospital using a fictitious name; doesn't write, phone, or tell any of her friends or family where she is. And gives birth to quintuplets.

I don't wanna brag, but my daughter is going with a professional man. A Notary Public!

If people walk all over you, have you ever considered a linoleum vest?

The fastest way to meet new people: Pick up somebody else's change at a bar.

You know what I think is the silliest response ever? "But my husband won't like it!" Especially when you're not asking her husband.

I've been reading that advice column for years and the way I figure it, the happiest person in the world must be Mr. Abby!

There are some things you're always a little suspicious of. Like a mortician who brings flowers.

They say baldness is an indication of masculinity. The only trouble is, it lessens your opportunities to prove it!

Love at first sight is that magic moment when you discover she has the same neuroses you do.

Everything is regulated these days. Even the Bluebird of Happiness is filing a flight plan!

I

INCOME TAX

Talk about things going up, if forty years ago you had invested in taxes, today you'd be rich!

April 15th is when the government spring cleans your wallet.

April 15th is when millions of American taxpayers have a rendez-vous with debt!

April 15th is when the whole country feels like a household product—Mr. Cleaned!

I got a friend named Sam Gross who's so conceited—when he does his income tax, he thinks Gross Income is a personalized return!

I get all confused by these phrases like "double taxation." Sounds like something they put on bras!

Your gross income is a figure halfway between what your wife tells her friends and what your boss thinks you're worth!

It's not whether you win or lose, but how you play the game. Now if we can only convince Internal Revenue!

I just saw a modern-day version of *Faust*. In the first act he sells his soul to the Devil. Then he spends the rest of the opera trying to convince Internal Revenue it was a long-term capital gain!

I got a cousin who was bragging he pulls down 50,000 a year—but he was shrewd. Internal Revenue said: "You pull down

50,000 a year?" He said: "Yup!" They said: "What do you do?"
He said: "I milk cows!"

Nerve? One year he tried to pay his income tax with Green
Stamps!

Income tax time is when accountants go out and buy the handy
six-pak—and it's aspirin!

I go to the world's wealthiest tax accountant. I'll tell you how
wealthy he is. He takes his vacation in March!

I get so upset by the income tax. Five minutes after I mail it in,
I offer to settle!

I know a kid who got very confused when he heard the phrase
"income tax." From listening to his father, he always thought
it had two words in front of it.

I don't wanna say anything about taxes, but last week I left my
heart in San Francisco and everything else at Internal Revenue!

You remember the Internal Revenue Service—the outfit that lives
for bread alone!

I don't mind the government pumping money into the economy
—but they always want to use my well!

I just saw a very touching sign. It said: PLEASE BE KIND TO THE
BARTENDER. HE UNDERESTIMATED HIS INCOME TAX TOO!

Yes, in the words of our kindly old neighborhood income tax
collector: " 'Tis better to give than to receive. And it's safer too!"

I'm so broke, my tax shelter has a second mortgage!

You know where we went wrong during the American Revolution? It should have been NO TAXATION WITH REPRESENTATION too!

INCOME TAX AUDIT

April 15th is one of our great religious holidays. Believe me, there are no atheists in the waiting room of the Internal Revenue Service!

I know a fella who got one of those calls from the Internal Revenue Service. They asked him to please come down and bring his records. So he did. He brought his Frank Sinatra records, his Barbra Streisand records.

I know another fella who got called down because he listed three blondes under Living Expenses. They asked him: "That's Living?" And he said: "You better believe it!"

They said: "Is this the first time you've been called down for this kind of an examination?" He said: "Yes it is. How could you tell?" They said: "You don't have to take off your clothes!"

One time I asked an auditor: "Who does *your* taxes?" He said: "A C.P.A. Who can understand this?"

INCOME TAX DEDUCTIONS

Did you hear about the guy who deducted $2000 because he had water in his basement? Then they found out he lived in a houseboat?

Then there's the architect who bought his wife a bra and deducted it from his income tax. Called it a Structural Improvement!

My impression of a fella toting up his church contributions for income tax purposes: "Well, I gave $2.00 last Sunday. Two dollars on Christmas. And $2.00 on Thanksgiving. That's $222.

Guts is playing around with a doctor's wife and listing it on your income tax as Medical Expenses!

INCOME TAX FORMS

Yes, it's income tax time again. When the government sends you those little booklets without any pictures.

This year the government claims the forms are so simple, even a three-year-old can understand them. Providing he's a C.P.A.

Every time I read the instructions for the income tax—it's almost like a religious experience. They passeth all understanding!

If you read the income tax instructions very carefully, you quickly realize there are only two ways to fill out the form—and they're both wrong.

I get so mad at the income tax, you know that box that says DO NOT WRITE IN THIS SPACE? I drop a big blob of chicken fat right in the middle. I figure if I can't write in that space—nobody else is gonna write in it either!

INDIA

Have you noticed how popular Indian music has become? Indian music is sort of a cross between Lawrence Welk and static.

It's amazing how many people are packing $10,000 worth of luggage; driving down to the airport in their Rolls-Royce; and flying first-class to India so they can meditate on the simple life.

When I was in India, I read with astonishment these never-to-be-forgotten words: "May the all-seeing eye dwelling in the treetop of infinite knowledge, bring its light of peace and understanding upon the tranquil meadows of the turbulent night of our hours of darkness!" Now I'll tell you why I was astonished. It was a bumper sticker!

Have you heard any of these Indian gurus who have something profound to say about everything? They're like a mother-in-law with a beard!

So many people are getting interested in Indian mysticism, the next *Playboy* centerfold will feature this beautiful naked girl—contemplating her staple!

Did you hear about the person who went to India and enrolled in that school that teaches the true meaning of life for $5000? It's called Guru U.

I just met the world's unhappiest guru. He has spent 32 years meditating—on why he has spent 32 years meditating!

I don't have to go to a guru to find inner peace. I take Tums!

INFLATION

There are a lot of things that money can't buy. For instance, what it did ten years ago.

Inflation is when your wife asks for a $20 bill to go shopping and you say: "Take two. They're small!"

It's such a wonderful feeling to go into a supermarket—get 25¢ off the same coffee you got 10¢ off the previous week—and still wind up paying the same price!

Inflation is when wallets are getting bigger and shopping bags are getting smaller.

Inflation is when "He who steals my purse" really does steal trash!

Inflation is when vegetarians aren't the only ones who don't eat meat!

Everybody's talking about inflation again. Inflation—that's when you pay a dime for nickel penny candy.

You know what inflation is. That's when the product you paid too much for in January is a bargain in April!

The way things are going, in 1980 Social Security will be $500 —and hamburgers $600!

Nowadays, I don't know anybody whose fixed income doesn't need repair work.

Remember the good old days—when shoes were elevated and prices weren't?

They say kids don't know the value of a dollar. They certainly do know the value of a dollar. That's why they ask for five!

I have a great idea to slow down inflation. We make it take the Long Island Expressway!

Have you heard the expression "as phony as a three dollar bill?" Let's just hope it won't apply to fives, tens, and twenties as well!

I just looked at a dollar bill and Washington has his fingers crossed!

It's ridiculous. I know a fella who inherited $100,000. He blew $5000 on the horses; $10,000 at Las Vegas; $15,000 on booze— and the rest he spent foolishly. Put it in the bank!

Inflation is now becoming such a serious problem, they ought to make banks put up a sign: SAVING MAY BE HAZARDOUS TO YOUR WEALTH!

INSULTS

I won't say she's fat but she gets fan letters from Captain Ahab!

I don't wanna wish this man any harm, but when my kids get up on Christmas morning, he should only be standing between them and the presents!

Anybody can make a mistake. He just happens to own the only typewriter in town with a key that says ooops!

HECKLER: I wish you only the best things in life. A lovely apartment in the nicest building in town. And in the apartment over yours—José Greco!

I won't say what (insert name) does to audiences but Brahms' "Lullabye" is getting jealous!

TO BAND: I'd like to pay you fellas what you're worth—but I don't wanna break the Minimum Wage Law.

It's kinda hard to describe these fellas. They've got a lot of polish, but it's all on their toenails.

I don't wanna complain about my wife, but right now she's taking a course in Remedial Sex.

INTERIOR DECORATORS

Even interior decorators have come up with a bumper sticker: PRAY FOR PUCE!

I just met the world's toughest interior decorator. He has six notches on his purse!

I don't wanna say anything, but this fella has all the sex drive of a whooping crane.

Show me a Communist sympathizer who's an interior decorator and I'll show you a finky pinky!

I guess you heard about that group of interior decorators who are getting together to form a voting bloc. It'll be called Fuchsia Power!

Did you hear about the interior decorator who became a trapeze artist, and one night the wind was blowing so bad he refused to go up without a net. The ringmaster said: "A safety net?" He said: "No, silly. A hairnet!"

INVENTIONS

What a great idea—a combination motel and delicatessen. It's for catered affairs!

Have you heard the latest? Fluoridated socks. You never get a hole in them!

Now there's a new product to protect your clothes. Moth balls and marijuana. One whiff and the moths just stand around snapping their fingers!

Those drug companies are really trying. One of them just brought out a product that's guaranteed to put you to sleep. Home movies!

I got an idea that's gonna make me a fortune! We mix Geritol with a detergent—for dirty old men!

I just thought of something that'll drive bees out of their mind! Arpège pollen!

I like to hear about things that shake up the world—like the caveman who invented the wheel asking General Motors for a royalty!

What a great idea. Fluoridated hair tonic for people with holes in their heads!

ISRAEL

Abbreviations mean different things in different countries. A sign in front of an American motel saying "TV" means television. In Israel it means Tourists Velcome!

It must be a terrible thing to read detective stories in Israel. Right away you know who the murderer is.

Superman is very big in this country and I understand Captain Marvel is a sensation in Israel. 'Cause they just found out "Shazam!" is "Matzohs" spelled backwards!

Is it true, if you're lost in the desert on the Gaza Strip—you're rescued by a St. Bernard dog with a keg of seltzer?

ITALY

I know a fella who's part Italian and part hairdresser. Sort of a Sissyilian.

There's a town in Italy that put up two high-rise cemeteries that hold 15,000 bodies. Isn't that great? If you really wanna be ostentatious, you get a vault with a terrace!

I think a high-rise cemetery is a wonderful idea. It's as close to Heaven as some of us are gonna get!

Who knows? Maybe this is Heaven. Two buildings—15,000 people —and nobody has to take out the garbage!

I just came across an incredible piece of information. How many people know the Lone Ranger was Italian? That's right. Couldn't speak a word of English. And you know *why* you didn't know? Because his horse Silver was three things—loyal, courageous, and a ventriloquist! . . . I didn't believe it myself until I saw their last picture. The opening scene gives it away. It shows the Lone Ranger talking to Tonto while Silver is drinking a glass of water!

It really must shake perfectionists—all this attention being given the Leaning Tower of Pisa.

According to a survey, there are one million prostitutes in Italy. These, of course, are loose figures.

Now I know what those girls in the travel agencies mean: SEVEN DAYS IN ITALY MAKE ONE WEAK!

My wife has one girdle—I think it's half nylon and half lead. Last year we were in Italy. Someone tried to pinch her and broke two fingers!

J

JANUARY

Here it is January again—when New England farmers think up all the funny things to say the *Reader's Digest* quotes in August.

January is when the entire country turns white—the land from snow falling down, and husbands from bills falling due!

January is when the 350-pound college football star of December joins the basketball team—as business manager.

January 1st is when every race horse in the country ages a year—and when some of the people who bet on them age ten!

I always feel good about the start of a new year. To many of us, January 1st is the eraser God provides to wipe the slate clean.

JOBS

If you're ever down and depressed, get out a copy of the last letter you wrote applying for a job, and you'll realize what an admirable person you are.

It's amazing how important your job is when you want the day off—and how unimportant it is when you want a raise.

So this machine operator comes home from the factory and tells his wife: "Sarah, I've got some good news and I've got some bad news. First, the good news: I got twenty-five thousand dollars severance pay." His wife said: "Twenty-five thousand dollars in severance pay? That's great! Now what's the bad news?" He said: "Wait'll you hear what was severed!"

I just met the world's hippest fortune teller. Reads the salt on Margaritas!

I know a fella who's making a fortune down in Alabama. He sells lobster bibs to short Ku Klux Klansmen!

I know an Indian who's making a fortune. He's a marriage counselor to interracial couples.

I had a terrible nightmare last night. I dreamt I sold electric blankets in Peyton Place!

People always jump to conclusions. Like I know a fella who's a stick-up man in an alley. He's a pin boy!

K

KARATE

Did you hear about the karate school that makes $100,000 a year by teaching people how to break boards with their hands—and another 2000 from selling kindling!

And Christmas is when karate experts face their greatest challenge! First they break a board in half. Then they break a brick in half. Then they tackle the hardest object of them all—a holiday fruit cake!

To me, karate doesn't make sense. You spend all your time hitting boards. And when was the last time you were attacked by a piece of wood?

The basic weapon in karate is the chop! (SLASH DOWN SHARPLY WITH HEEL OF HAND) Then there's the Greenwich Village version of the chop: (LEFT HAND ON HIP AND PUSH AWAY WITH YOUR RIGHT HAND). That doesn't really hurt your opponent, but the breeze might give him a cold!

I got a great idea for an up-dated version of *Don Quixote*. You know that scene where Don Quixote attacks the windmill? In my version, he uses karate!

Optimism is a karate expert going up to a Sequoia.

KU KLUX KLAN

I don't know why they say the South isn't making progress. I just saw a Klansman wearing a mini-sheet!

The Ku Klux Klan is very big. Kids run around in funny costumes on Halloween and their parents do it the rest of the year!

It's amazing the way the Ku Klux Klan is keeping up with the times. Like they just started a Negro Auxiliary.

Did you hear about the KKK member whose wife got a divorce? One night he came home wearing a different sheet!

L

LAWNS

Anyone who uses the expression "dirt cheap" has never gone out and bought topsoil.

Home owners are people who invest hundreds of dollars in mulch, nutrients, and fertilizer—and then get mad 'cause they have to cut the grass. . . . It's called PAY AS YOU MOW!

I've seen stretches of 9 by 12 lawn that could have been carpeted cheaper!

And if you don't have an 8-cylinder power lawn mower—don't show up at the next P.T.A. meeting. You'll be pointed to death!

I just bought a power lawn mower and I have only one question: Are toes good for mulch?

I've had so little come up, I'm even grateful for crab grass!

I don't know why crab grass should be crabby. It's always winning!

But then when everything is perfect. The lawn is trimmed, manicured, a velvety green. The garden is ablaze with color and the hammock is ready. Well, you know what happens then. You all pack up, go away to the country, and you never see it again till Labor Day!

I'm the suspicious type. Like, I *know* why the grass is always greener in the other fellow's yard. Spray paint!

Now comes the summertime. The blood and sweat is over and

all you've got left is the tears—when you see the size of the water bill.

I don't mind playing wet nurse to a lawn—but my liquor bill isn't as high as *its* water bill! . . . And what makes it even worse, I got a lot higher than it ever did!

Lawns are the passion of suburbanites. I think after that long trip home each night, they don't have energy for anything else!

M

MARRIAGE

Are you living a life of *quiet* desperation—or are you married?

The big question most husbands have to decide is—are they a man or a spouse?

I won't say I'm henpecked, but I even had to play my cards right on the honeymoon!

One wedding was so posh, at the head table they had a figure of the bride carved in ice. Everybody thought it was sculpture. Later on it proved to be prophecy!

I wouldn't say she's frigid. Let's just say she flunked puberty!

It was a double-ring ceremony. Well, most weddings are double-ring ceremonies. One around the bride's finger and one through the groom's nose.

I won't say how the honeymoon went, but when they came down to the breakfast room he asked for separate checks.

Did you hear about the newlywed who's working a five-day weak?

Did you hear about the couple who got married and had eight kids—in rabbit succession?

They say marriages are made in Heaven—and Reno is where they're called back for repairs!

Marriage—that's a love-in with a license!

A husband is a person who is under the impression he bosses the house—when in reality, he only houses the boss.

You know what's wrong with the world today? People are adding love to dog food when it's marriages that need it!

A domestic quarrel is when she says: "I'm so upset, I'm going to a headshrinker!" And he says: "It ain't your head that needs shrinking. It's your mouth!"

You know you've made a bad marriage if you go in for wife-swapping—and have to throw in the upstairs maid!

I don't wanna complain, but did you see my wife's letter in Dear Abby this morning? It said: "Dear Abby: Until I got married, I didn't realize Brand X made husbands!"

Marriage is the only institution that doesn't allow you to hire summer help.

Believe me, you can get in a lot of trouble through a misunderstanding. Especially if your Mrs. doesn't!

The happiest man I know is a husband who plays around with a girl called Passion Flower DeBoys. 'Cause once a week he can go up to his wife, look her straight in the eye and say: "Honey, I'm going out with DeBoys!"

I know a fella who's gone bowling every Saturday night for the last ten years—and his wife's so trusting, she still thinks you do it in a tux.

I wouldn't call him a chaser. Let's just say he's an underachiever!

Shrewd? For her birthday, he gave his wife a gift subscription— to *Playboy*.

MEDICINE

Nowadays you don't have to worry about things like colds. You can take pills to eliminate nasal congestion; pills to counteract the symptoms of sore throat, coughs, and headaches; pills to give you quick energy and increase your body tone and vigor. Thanks to medical science, every day people are dying who never looked better!

The way I see it—a miracle drug is anything that'll do 25 per cent of the things the label says it will.

"Did you hear about Mrs. Jones? She's trying artificial insemination—the hard way."
"The hard way?"
"She's having an affair with a robot!"

Scientists are now on the brink of making one of the greatest medical discoveries of all time—fluoridated chicken soup!

The way Medicare is going, I would guess that in 1975 it will pay for dentists; in 1980 it will pay for psychiatrists; and in 1985 it will pay for get-well cards!

Sometimes I wonder if the Democrats didn't make a big mistake pushing through Medicare. I know a fella who's gotten so many free tranquilizers—he doesn't care who he votes for!

"George is a man of many parts."
"Versatility?"
"No. Transplants!"

It shows you the progress we've made. Ten years ago an organ transplant would have been a Hammond going from one church to another.

Each week, science learns a little more about how to create life. Kinda makes you wonder if God has Social Security.

Personally, I always go to (insert name) Hospital, 'cause that's where all the truck drivers get operated on.

I understand what an ulcer is but what's a peptic? Sounds like an energetic twitch!

MEN'S CHARACTER

Bashful? He's the type who would steal a kiss at an orgy!

Everything happens to me. I mean, who else ever got a threatening phone call—from Information?

My memory is so bad, I'm the only one who can watch *Hamlet* and not know who the murderer is!

Nerve? They just finished a movie about him: COME WIZ ME TO ZE CHUTZPAH!

He's the type who likes to bug people. Like yesterday he wrote to the Encyclopedia Britannica people and asked them when it was coming out in paperback.

Extravagant? This man just spent $5000 to have his teeth capped —and they were false!

He's just naturally evil. You know that toothpaste test on TV? He pulls for the cavities!

He's the type who goes in for strange practical jokes—like serving that Army coffee at drive-in movies.

He's the kind of fella who'd go to a night club with a show featuring Frank Sinatra, Bob Hope, Barbra Streisand, and Herb Alpert—and complain about the relief band.

This guy is such a phony, even when he gives you cash it's post-dated.

I won't say this man lies—but in the Army of Truth, he is definitely A.W.O.L.

Lazy? You know those cold remedies that let you sleep for eight hours? He takes two of them.

Square? He's the type who talks louder on long distance calls.

I won't say what his parents think of him, but he is an only child.

Dumb? He thinks charisma is a Mexican curse!

This fella is so wild, LSD takes him!

He's the kind of a guy who cheats at Monopoly. That's right. Uses loaded hotels!

Unlucky? You're looking at the only fella who ever found a four-leaf poison ivy!

I know a fella who's so unpopular—yesterday he joined a key club and this morning they changed the locks!

Cheap? If he was at the Last Supper, he would have asked for separate checks!

I just met the world's nerviest person. Makes obscene phone calls —collect!

He's got some odd ideas—like turning the Pennsylvania Turnpike into a play street.

I won't say he's a pessimist, but the only thing he expects to get on a silver platter is tarnish.

Shallow? If it wasn't for bumper stickers, he wouldn't have any opinions at all!

I know a fellow who lives such a dog's life, he has special car insurance. Not for driving them—for chasing them!

I'm so unlucky, if I invested in a guitar factory—jug blowing would come back!

But he's really a wonderful man. If I asked for it, he'd give me the shirt off his back. Why not? It's mine!

MEN'S CLOTHES

Is it my imagination, or are they putting more pins in new shirts? I took one apart last night—and it was like committing hara-kiri on the installment plan!

When it comes to wardrobe, I'm sort of a progressive conservative. Like I wear turtle-neck shirts—but with a tie!

Have you tried to buy a pair of socks lately? They only come in one size—stretch! . . . Stretch socks are a modern invention whereby one sock fits every size foot the same way—badly!

Did you ever have one of those terrible days? This morning, the permanent crease in my pants came out.

And now they've come up with mini-pants for men. It's fascinating. They look like jockey shorts with a crease!

I dunno. Did you ever get the feeling while looking at mini-skirts and mini-pants—that Berkeley is winning?

Thanks to mini-pants, for the first time in history, men are faced with the same leg problems as women: To shave or not to shave! In fact, there's a new electric razor on the market—the Lady Sam!

I'll never forget the first time I wore a pair of mini-pants. People kept saying: "That's the living end!" And they were right. The belt broke!

Is it true the Supreme Court is wearing mini-robes?

I once tried on a pair of paper shorts, but never again. I didn't mind the rattling. I didn't mind the crinkling. But man, those splinters were murder!

The problem with paper shorts is you gotta have a paper belt to go with them. Otherwise, they're known as U.F.O.s—Unidentified Falling Objects!

MIDDLE AGE

Middle age is when your brain says: "Go! Go! Go!"—while the rest of you is saying: "No! No! No!"

I may be forty, but every morning when I get up, I feel like a twenty year old. Unfortunately, there's never one around!

Forty is a ridiculous age to be. You're too young to be called old and too old to be called young. You're a 'tween-ager!

Middle age is when a night on the town is followed by two on your back.

Middle age is that terrible feeling that comes over you when you say to a kid: "What do you mean: 'What's a running board?'"

MIDWEST

A survey shows that "adult" movies are very unpopular in Iowa. I've lived in farm country. Maybe they just don't want to make sex a spectator sport!

But you have to admire the people in Iowa for being strong-minded. This is the only state where they use the backs of French postcards for shopping lists!

They just don't want to know about these things. In Iowa, a stripper is a bacon slicer!

I kinda suspected something like this when a house of ill repute had to take out a second mortgage!

Personally, I have always been intrigued by Cincinnati. No matter how you spell it, it always looks wrong.

They say it took the pioneers two months to go from the Mississippi River to California. You can still do it. Let your wife read the road map!

MILLIONAIRES

I just saw the world's rarest sight. Avon calling and Howard Hughes answering!

Wouldn't it be funny if there were no such person as Howard Hughes? That it was just swamp gas?

Can you imagine if J. Paul Getty ever became a hippie? He'd be the first hippie whose thing was 2 billion dollars!

Never mind the jet set. I just want to be a member of that group that has ten million dollars in the bank—the set set!

Important? He gets calendars from the World Bank!

It's not that he always sides with big business. Let's just say that his main concern is with the uptrodden of the world.

Rich? He sends gift certificates to Howard Hughes!

MINI-SKIRTS

MINI-SKIRT: a Freudian slip.

No, a Freudian slip is when your secretary comes into the office wearing a mini-skirt and you say: "Thigh, there!"

I'm not surprised that girls are wearing mini-skirts. The way fellas are wearing their hair, they gotta do something to look different.

Wouldn't it be scary if there were no such thing as mini-skirts? Girls are just getting taller?

Wait'll you see what women are wearing this spring—micro-skirts! That's jockey shorts with a hem!

And now they're talking about an outfit that's 10 inches *below* the knee. It's called a meany-skirt.

Thanks to mini-skirts, for the first time in history panty raids are beginning to make sense!

Did you hear about the girl who wore a mini-skirt out in the rain—and it shrank something wonderful?

Now they're talking about dropping mini-skirts. Is there no modesty at all?

It's easy for a girl to be in style these days. All she needs is a mini-skirt and maxi-nerve.

Do you realize if mini-skirts get any shorter, women will *have* to wear the pants in the family?

There was this news story that hemlines are now 3 inches above the knee in Russia. 'Course, I won't say what the legs on Russian women look like—but one of them was just attacked by a piano!

MODERN LIVING

Modern living is really wonderful. You get ptomaine and you have your choice of who to charge it to: Medicare, Blue Cross, or the Diner's Club.

You know what our big problem today is? We've run out of slogans. REMEMBER THE ALAMO! REMEMBER THE MAINE! REMEMBER PEARL HARBOR! What have we got to remember today? Our zip code!

I'm so weary. They expect me to remember my zip code, my area code, my phone number, my Social Security number. Are they kidding? I still write "1970" on checks!

People are so confused these days. You'd be surprised how many people get in a cab and give the driver their zip code.

Did you read about that outfit that freezes bodies? I don't wanna complain, but I think my wife joined it.

If you think everything these days is coin-operated, ask your teen-ager to shovel snow for a quarter.

This is a time of suspicion. Teen-agers don't trust anyone over 30 and Meter Maids don't trust anyone over 60.

Why even in King Arthur's time they had key clubs. They were called chastity belts!

I just figured out the group that's behind all those dry cleaners who staple tags into your clothes. Manicurists!

If ever you feel neglected and depressed because no one writes to you, follow this one simple suggestion: Subscribe to five major magazines; let the subscriptions expire—and don't renew . . . . At 60¢ a hundred pounds, you can retire on the waste paper alone!

MODERN MUSIC

I've been listening to some of the new songs and believe me, never before has Tin Pan sounded so much like an Alley!

If you don't think there's a generation gap—remember when three little words meant: "I Love You?" Now it's : "Yeah! Yeah! Yeah!"

And some of these rock-and-roll groups are pretty wild. First time I ever saw a switchblade guitar!

Now they've got a stereo that gives real concert-hall sound. Every two minutes it coughs and rattles a program.

Have you noticed how war songs have changed? Remember the big war song of 1942—"Goodbye Mama, I'm Off To Yokohama?" Why that song made millions of Americans fighting mad! Not soldiers—music lovers!

I just saw a startling statistic. That every day in the United States, 800 million pounds of garbage is created—and that's not even counting rock-and-roll records!

Somehow it seems wrong to have a record listing called the TOP FORTY and not have Racquel Welch on it.

There's one thing that bothers me about playing the bagpipes. How do you know when you've hit a wrong note?

You gotta be impressed with the size of some of these singing groups. One of them has 42 people. It's so big, three of them are listeners!

Nowadays, if you get the D.T.s—you don't know whether to get a doctor and get cured—or a guitar and get rich!

Maybe it's a good thing Wolfgang Amadeus Mozart isn't making records today. How would they get a name like that on a 45?

I'm not knocking rock and roll, but if Van Gogh were alive today, he'd cut off both ears!

I love to listen to those Country and Western bands down in Louisiana. I mean, where else can you hear a cowbell solo?

We may laugh at these rock-and-roll singers with the long, dirty hair, but some of them carry a tremendous load on their shoulders—dandruff!

You know what's wrong with the world today? Guns have silencers when it's electric guitars that need them!

MONEY

Show me the father who reaches into his pocket to give his son an advance on next month's allowance—and I'll show you a grave digger!

I'm so confused by all this hippie talk, when I give my teen-ager his allowance I mark it FOREIGN AID!

Isn't it frightening how fast later comes, after you buy now?

You know what's wrong with this country? We're putting Platformate in our gasoline to make it go further—when it's our money that needs it!

Wouldn't that be a wonderful name for a fella who's always borrowing money till payday? Kort Short!

It's really fantastic how far this credit card craze has gone. Last night, there was a fella in here who wanted to pay in cash and they wouldn't take it—until he showed his Diner's Club Card as a reference.

The greatest paradox of our time: If you want a thicker wallet, take all the credit cards out of it.

I don't worry about money. My wife wanted a foreign convertible —I got her one. A rickshaw.

If you feel money is the root of all evil, call me in. I'm your friendly Roto-rooter man!

Most people would be satisfied with enough, if others didn't have more.

Rich? He has so many government bonds—if he ever cashed them in, the country would bounce!

The way I look at money, you can't take it with you. And even if you could, it would have to be fireproof!

Do you realize if collectors keep paying more for Confederate dollar bills—and inflation keeps taking away from regular dollar bills—the South won't *have* to rise again?

You can always tell the people who say: "Money can't buy happiness." They're the ones who usually have had very little experience with either.

And they're wrong. Money *can* buy happiness. Ask anyone who subscribes to *Playboy!*

Let's face it, there's only one thing money can't buy—poverty! . . . You need the stock market to do that!

Did you hear about the South American dictator who keeps having this terrible nightmare—that his wife goes up to the withdrawal window in a Swiss bank and says: "I'm Mrs. 374869!"

MOTHER-IN-LAW

We now have a law that prohibits outside agitators from crossing state lines. I sent a copy of it to my mother-in-law!

And New Year's Day is when everybody goes visiting. My mother-in-law came over last New Year's Day and had a wonderful time. She must have. She never left!

And subtlety doesn't help. Like yesterday we did over the room in a brand new style—Early Roadmap!

Until I met my mother-in-law, I didn't realize there was a Mrs. Scrooge!

MOVIES

Hollywood is now making a Western that's so modern, the Indian medicine man is a pediatrician!

The next Hollywood trend will be realistic religious pictures. Moses on Mount Sinai looking up from his stone tablets and yelling: "Not so fast! Not so fast!"

Personally, I always enjoy the big spectacles. Where they spend so much money to buy the stars, the sets, the costumes, and 10,000 extras—they don't have anything left over for a plot!

As Robert E. Lee said when they announced this latest reissue of *Gone with the Wind:* "You people sure know how to hurt a fella!"

They say an Oscar is worth one million dollars to the winning picture. Maybe they ought to call them the Academy Rewards.

And this year, they came up with some unusual nominations. Like for the Best Supporting Role for the Year—Maidenform!

Did you know the Supreme Court won't let them hold the Academy Award program in a public school? Too much praying going on!

I love to watch late night TV, with all those wonderful movies and variety acts. Last night *The General Died At Dawn* along with three comics!

In the thirties, you could see two of these movies for a dime. Now it costs you $500 for a TV set and what do you see? Those same movies!

The thirties were when Jimmy Cagney was the toughest guy in the movies. Remember Jimmy Cagney? He was sort of a bonsai John Wayne!

In one of his pictures, Jimmy Cagney shoved a grapefruit into a girl's face, and it was called shocking. Now it's called a diet!

In the thirties they also made those wonderful pictures with hundreds of beautiful dancing girls—at least two of whom could.

And tap-dancing was very big. Every movie had eight big production numbers; eight incredible sets; eight lavish costume changes; one time step!

One actress got to be a star because she had three variations on the time step: slow, fast, and uncertain!

And you can't imagine the costumes. Do you know I was eighteen before I realized show girls didn't grow sequins?

Some of these girls were so loaded with glitter the actors didn't know whether to kiss them or pawn them!

I never had much luck in show business. Like, thirty years ago I lost my shirt on a team called Astaire and Rogers. Ginger Astaire and Fred Rogers!

N

NEW MORALITY

You know what's wrong with the world today? Movies have signs saying: ADULTS ONLY—when it's maternity hospitals that need them!

It's embarrassing. In high schools all over the country, girls are graduating magna cum pregnant!

You can't imagine all the babies that are coming into this world breakfast-cereal style. They have snap, crackle, but no Pop!

And teen-age mothers have a problem. One of them is so young, when she called up the doctor about diaper rash, he said: "Whose?"

But you can't blame it all on the kids. A lot of teen-agers are in trouble because of the group they hang out with. Their parents!

One Hollywood kid is now working on his fifth father by his fourth mother! . . . And I'll say one thing for him. He never talks back to his dad. Why should he? He hardly knows the man!

They say that 45 per cent of the colleges and universities are handing out birth-control information. And the rest are handing out diapers!

According to the experts, when it comes to sex, too many kids start experimenting with their fingers crossed—which is the wrong part.

It's a problem. Some girls are graduating from college with an M.A.—and others are graduating from college *as* an MA!

In fact, in colleges today there's a new definition of an honor student. That's one who passes tests—final, toothpaste, and Wasserman!

According to the latest surveys, nude swimming is now the fastest growing outdoor sport in America. It's called Skinny Dipping or Keeping Up with the Joneses.

You can tell the people who practice it. They invite 2 couples over and put out 32 hangers.

I can remember when you went to a party—ate, drank, talked, drove home, undressed, and went to bed. Nowadays people do the same things only it's not in that order!

Let's face it, there are some things that just won't make it in this world—like skinny dipping in Alaska.

Misery is a skinny dipper who's nearsighted.

"The problem with the world today is sex. People are drenched in novels about sex, films about sex, lectures about sex. Advertising is based on sex. Schools have sex education courses. We're becoming obsessed with sex, sex, sex! Now, what do you have to say about that?" "Your place or mine?"

NEW YEAR'S EVE

New Year's Eve is when everybody cries a little. I think it's throwing away that *Playboy* Calendar.

On New Year's Eve I like to call up different friends around the country, but it's always so confusing with the different times. Like last year, I was talking to an operator in New York and I said: "How far behind New York is Los Angeles?" She said: "Literally or culturally?"

I have one big problem with New Year's Eve. I misplace things. Like New Year's Day.

New Year's Eve is when everybody in show business works. I saw one stripper who was so old, she had two problems in taking it off. The law and arthritis.

I had a terrible fight with my wife on New Year's Eve. She called me a procrastinator. So I stopped addressing Christmas cards and left!

Frankly, I don't mind being called a procrastinator. I mean—if you're going to crastinate, be good at it!

More and more, when you say: "Happy New Year!"—it's a triumph of hope over experience.

NEW YEAR'S EVE—DRINKING

I'm a little worried about my diet. I drank a quart of eggnog. Tell me. How many calories is cinnamon?

You remember eggnog. The drink that gives you a big head and a stomach to match?

Have you ever tasted eggnog? It's like drinking milk from a smashed cow!

Eggnog is half cream and half booze. Sort of a Mootini.

What do you call it when you get stinking drunk? A Hippie New Year!

Mark my words, on New Year's Eve you'll find LSD on every corner—Large Sloppy Drunks!

I had a terrible experience on New Year's Eve. I got drunk and they tried to sober me up with Irish coffee!

I won't say what I walked home on, but I had athlete's knees!

My neighbors never even go out on New Year's Eve. They do all their drinking at home. They figure the family that sways together, stays together!

And the husband loves to throw confetti. You know confetti. It looks like dandruff for color TV!

You should have seen him. All night long, throwing confetti into the air and yelling: "Happy New Year!" The next morning I went over and here's his wife, on her hands and knees, picking up those millions of little bits of paper off the floor. I said: "Did you have a Happy New Year?" She said: "*He* had a Happy New Year. To me it's Labor Day!"

NEW YEAR'S EVE—DRIVING

I'd like to say just one thing for New Year's Eve. If you drive on the Freeways, don't drink. 'Cause those rest stops are pretty far apart!

I'll never forget one New Year's Eve. The National Safety Council *over*estimated by 75 accidents. My wife didn't take out the car.

The National Safety Council is really great. This year they have a special warning just for people who own pools: IF YOU DRINK, DON'T DIVE!

I used to call my car Old Acquaintance 'cause every New Year's Eve I forgot where I parked it!

NEW YEAR'S EVE—PARTIES

With all the eating and guzzling and boozing, New Year's Eve is when you appreciate the truly thoughtful hostess. The one who puts out bicarbonate cheese dip!

Once upon a time, this fella went to a New Year's Eve costume party by himself because his wife wasn't feeling well. And he met this mysterious masked woman. He wined with her; he dined with her; he danced with her; he romanced with her; he suggested they run away to Las Vegas for the week end. And just then it was midnight. He pulled off his mask. She pulled off her mask— and it was his wife! And they both laughed—once upon a time.

I'm a conservative. When I go to one of those New Year parties where you have to bring a bottle—mine is aspirin!

Anything goes on New Year's Eve. It's when old acquaintance are forgot—along with hats, coats, and wives.

I won't say how much kissing goes on at midnight, but at 11:55 there's a coast to coast run on Sen-Sen!

Did we have a party! I walked up to one girl and said: "Would you like to dance?" She said: "I'd love to." I said: "I know, but my wife only lets me dance!"

Everybody was drinking illegitimate champagne. It didn't have any pop!

NEW YORK CITY

New Yorkers are so impersonal, if it wasn't for muggings there wouldn't be any contact at all!

I went to one of those outdoor cafés in New York and it was fascinating. First time I was ever mugged by a bus boy!

The smog over New York is so bad, skywriters no longer use smoke. They use oxygen!

The smog was so bad in Central Park, it's the first time I ever saw a Seeing Eye mugger!

But smog is nothing new. New York even had air pollution back in 1609. That's how Staten Island got its name. Henry Hudson sailed into Lower New York Bay—peered through the smog, and said: "Is Staten Island?"

For years New Yorkers have been making fun of the Los Angeles smog. Well now they're coughing out of the other side of their mouths!

They're even writing songs about the smog. Like: "I wonder who's kissing me now?"

Not to overlook: "A smoggy day in New York town; it turned my lungs, from pink to brown!"

I like New York. Where else can you see someone invest in a Mutual Fund with a welfare check?

While attending some of these off-Broadway plays—did you ever get the feeling that the author's previous experience was writing dialogue for obscene phone calls?

I saw one play. I didn't know if they were reading the script or the men's room wall!

NIGHT CLUBS

What a great sign for a night club: IF YOU LIVED HERE, YOU'D BE STONED NOW.

The worst part of spending $45 for an evening out—when you come home, the baby-sitter usually looks like she had a better time than you did.

I won't say the liquor in this place is watered—but if you want a chaser, they give you a double!

An art school is looking for people who can draw. So are night-club owners.

NONSENSE JOKES

I know a fella who only goes to nudist camps for the comedians.

I like the song about that kid who keeps failing in school 'cause he stays out all night: "I hate to see that evening son go down."

Who shall ever forget those immortal words the Devil spoke after Faust sold him his soul: "No Green Stamps?"

I tell you, this wife-swapping has gone too far. I just saw Hansel and Jill go into the forest and Jack and Gretel go up the hill!

Show me a fella who likes to sleep twelve hours a day and I'll show you a bed bug!

Wouldn't that make a wonderful prize for the kid who delivers the most copies of the Sunday newspaper? A cowboy hernia belt!

Show me the man who doesn't know the meaning of the word "fear"—and I'll show you a prospect for a Webster's Unabridged Dictionary!

I'm fascinated by that house down the street with the little green light out in front. I figure it's either an Irish bawdy house or an unmarked police station.

I know a fella who's thankful because so many of our cups runneth over. He's a dry cleaner!

SING: Nobody knows the trouble I've seen. Nobody knows but Dear Abby!

People who live in glass houses, shouldn't move to Peyton Place!

It just isn't right—like a hearse with white sidewalls.

I tell you, this equal rights for women has gone too far. Yesterday a sorority went out on a jockey-shorts raid!

One girls' dormitory has had so many raids they're calling it the Pantygone.

Personally, I could never understand panty raids. A panty is like a Christmas stocking. Means nothing unless it's filled!

Is it true that in South Carolina, it's known as *The Christian Science Merrimac?*

It doesn't make sense, like playing Strip Solitaire.

Did you hear about the shoe-repair shop that has written across its window: SOLE BROTHER?

Friends—do you suffer from acid indigestion? So, who told you to drink acid?

I just joined that organization that fights moral decay the same way you fight tooth decay. You give your girl friend the brush after every meal!

You can always tell the people who eat week-old bagels. They have 31 per cent fewer teeth!

They say a diamond is the hardest substance on this earth. Have you ever tried frozen peanut butter on a stale bagel?

I don't wanna start any rumors, but you know the Jolly Green Giant wears elevator shoes!

If sex is supposed to be one of the driving forces in the world today —how come so much of it goes on in parked cars?

Take my advice, don't ever buy a cheap sun lamp. It doesn't pay. If you get caught in the rain, your tan runs!

Have you noticed how nobody complains about the price of stamps? That bourbon-flavored glue does it all the time!

It must be wonderful to go to an Ivy League college. Where else can you see kids writing on washroom walls in Latin?

Personally, I've never liked the Amazon. If there's one thing I can't stand it's a big mouth river! . . . I dunno. My geography teacher loved it!

NURSERY SCHOOL

I send my four-year-old to a day school and he just loves finger painting. Yesterday he painted one of them blue, another one red, another one—.

And today was the crowning achievement of them all—he learned to tie his shoelaces! To each other. . . . He's probably the only four year old in the world who minces.

I don't see it as a choice. Either we put three- and four-year-olds into schools—or they put their mothers into strait jackets.

NURSES

All over the country you read about nurses going on strike and walking out. What I wanna know is—how can they tell?

They call nurses Angels of Mercy. They must be angels—you never see them!

I was in a hospital last month and I won't say how many times I saw the nurse, but we used to call her Florence Nightingone!

That's right. The nurses in this hospital fell into three categories —GONE, GOING, and OFF DUTY!

But so you shouldn't feel alone, every bed has a buzzer. And it's very efficient. You ring once if you need something; you ring twice if you need something immediately; and you ring three times if it's too late!

But it's obvious, nurses have a lot of valid complaints. Like, I don't think they should be called Registered Nurses—unless they're planning to breed them!

Then there's another group called Practical Nurses. A Practical Nurse is one who's looking for another job.

But when it comes to pay scales, vacations, and fringe benefits— nurses are usually behind. At least that's where I've always found them.

O

OLD AGE

An old-timer is one who remembers when "Five and Ten" stood for cents instead of dollars.

There's only one problem with going through a second childhood. This time you can't blame your troubles on your parents!

I think my father-in-law is going through his second childhood. He just put braces on his plates!

It's kind of a shame that just when you learn to make the best of life—the best is mostly gone.

It's an awful thing to grow old by yourself. My wife hasn't had a birthday in seven years!

My wife is something. She never lies about her age. She just tells everyone she's as old as I am. Then she lies about my age.

P

PERSONALITIES

They say Richard Burton has a Rolls-Royce, a 100-foot yacht, a twin-engine jet plane, a few million dollars, and Liz Taylor. Sure. Sure. But is he happy?

People are always complaining about Phyllis Diller's hairdresser. What about Smokey the Bear's tailor?

You can't even call what Phyllis Diller has, a hair-do. It's more like a hair-don't!

Picture shredded wheat with bobby pins!

You don't know what it's like, hearing a bottle of peroxide say: "Are you kidding? Me—go into *that?*"

They say a woman is nothing but a rag, a bone, and a hank of hair. And in Phyllis Diller's case, that's overselling!

People keep talking about the Credibility Gap. For those of you who don't know what a Credibility Gap is—it's Phyllis Diller buying a C Cup!

Did you know that Phyllis Diller was once voted Miss America? Not by us—by the Russians!

It's kind of a shame about Phyllis Diller. Phyllis Diller looks the way every other American woman does at six o'clock in the morning—only she gets blamed for it!

You know who I love? Julie Andrews! This girl is so sweet, so charming, so agreeable. I know a husband who saw Julie Andrews —went home—tried to put out the garbage—but his wife didn't wanna go!

But I'm all confused by a name like "Julie." Where I come from, the only one who had a name like Julie was the bookie.

I really admire Frank Sinatra. He's so ring-a-ding-ding! I don't wanna brag, but I used to be ring-a-ding-ding. Until one day it happened—my ring-a-ding done dang!

I love to hear William Buckley talk. This man uses four syllables even when he burps!

My wife has lost 5 pounds just from reading Buckley's newspaper column. The dictionary is upstairs!

"Did you hear that Twiggy just got a big job in a library?" "Is she a librarian?" "No. A bookmark!"

Remember the good old days before Twiggy—when if girls wore padded bras, what they were padded with was girls!

Incidentally, there is no truth to the rumor that Twiggy has just been made the symbol for National Pancake Month!

She has an interesting figure. It's called Early Famine.

Her measurements are 31-22-32—in any order!

Believe me, a model who weighs 91 pounds doesn't have an easy time of it. She has to worry about long hours, bright lights, and strong vacuum cleaners!

She may be thin, but you'll never forget what she puts into a bra— her shoulder blades!

This is the only girl who has to wear falsies just to look flat-chested!

I just figured out what Twiggy reminds me of. A sex goddess for Don Knotts!

I love the way she poses with those knockwurst knees. One is knocked and the other is worse.

Guess who was just voted Man of the Year? Twiggy!

PETS

I just found out why you never hear about St. Bernard dogs anymore. Twenty years ago, one of them figured out how to get the cork out of the keg.

I won't say my wife is a kill-joy, but she just had our goldfish fixed!

You think you have troubles. I've got a parakeet who lisps!

PHILOSOPHY

Sometimes I get the feeling the winds of change have turned into a hurricane.

One of the nicest things about conscience is—it's on your side. It never bothers you until you've had your fun.

If you can keep your head while all others around you are losing theirs—get somebody to explain the situation to you.

If at first you don't succeed—try reading the instructions.

Instead of cursing the darkness, I lit one small candle! And my fire insurance rate went up 40 per cent!

Experience is the stuff that when you finally get enough of, you're too old to qualify for the job.

The man who can smile while everything about him is going wrong —was probably quitting anyway.

Live every day as if it were your last—and it soon will be!

Behind many a successful man in this world, there's a woman—and behind her, his wife!

Personally, I always tell my troubles to my enemies. They're the only ones who really want to hear them.

There's no question that variety is the spice of life. Too bad it takes monotony to finance it.

When you're invited to an evening of wine, women, and song—it sometimes pays to find out the vintage of the first two.

Always be wary of the fella who says you can't take it with you —'cause he's planning to take yours with him.

I take a philosophical attitude about necking. Like—getting there is half the fun!

Happiness is a comparison shopper at orgies!

They say in Asia, the navel is very important. They contemplate their navel and they find peace, tranquility, a transcendental awareness of being. I do the same darn thing, and all I ever find is lint!

One of the great truths I've discovered is that the world isn't waiting for the sunrise. The only ones waiting for the sunrise are night watchmen!

People who say nothing is impossible should try gargling with their mouths closed.

And they're always thinking deep thoughts. Yesterday one hippie said: "Life is like six frozen matzoth balls floating in a bowl of Kool-

Aid!" Another hippie asked him: "Why is life like six frozen matzoth balls floating in a bowl of Kool-Aid?" The first one said: "Hey, man. Did you come here to learn or argue?"

If at first you don't succeed—try listening to your wife.

Life begins at forty—if you think rheumatism is living.

If there were anything to this theory of evolution—by now, fish would be coming out of the water and trying again!

PHYSICAL FITNESS

I can remember when I used to laugh at life. Now I gotta rest up a week just to giggle a little.

Did you hear about the world's strongest lion tamer? Doesn't carry a chair—a couch!

People are always saying "Health is Wealth!" I got an uncle who doesn't think health is wealth. He's a mortician!

It doesn't make sense—like a vegetarian going to a barbecue.

THE PILL

Is it true they're now working on a special version of the Pill for teen-agers? It's chocolate flavored!

I wish women wouldn't keep referring to the Pill. You're never quite sure if they mean birth control or their husbands.

I know a woman who got to enjoy the Pill. Used to eat them like candy. One day she sneezed—sterilized her whole bridge club!

Eleven million women in the world use birth-control pills. They are called progressive. One billion women don't use birth-control pills. They are called Mama!

Wouldn't that make a wonderful name for a birth-control pill? STOP YOUR KIDDING!

They keep coming up with new birth-control ideas. Now there's a plan that calls for taking 200 little round pills a day. Then when you climb into bed, you roll right out again!

As a public service, I'd like to show you the lastest development in birth-control pills: (HOLD UP A BASKETBALL PAINTED WHITE). By the time your wife swallows it, you have to go to work!

PLANNED OBSOLESCENCE

Manufacturers are now going to tell consumers how long an appliance will last. Two minutes longer than the final payment!

This is called Planned Obsolescence, and it's really not a new concept. God used it with people.

That's the problem nowadays. Obsolescence is planned and adolescents aren't.

The whole idea of Planned Obsolescence is that nothing is made to last. Nothing! Automobiles, washing machines, marriages, or money!

I bought a toaster that was so shoddy the warranty was in disappearing ink!

I put in 2 slices of bread, and after 5 minutes they still came out white. And this was pumpernickel!

I was watching a Western on my new color TV. I don't wanna complain about the workmanship, but it's the first time I ever saw a wagon train attacked by green men!

And whenever I need a ball-point pen, I get three of them. One for smudging; one for tapping on the paper; and one for throwing away!

I don't know why they call them ball-point pens. Every one I have is a balled-up-point pen!

Be honest now. When was the last time you had a ball-point pen that worked? Believe me, if the Declaration of Independence had been signed with ball-point pens—we'd still be a colony!

PLAYBOY

Remember all those fellas who used to go to burlesque shows for the comics? They now read *Playboy* for the Party Jokes page.

If *Playboy* were smart, they'd have more Chinese Playmates of the Month—'cause after an hour, you feel like looking again.

What do you call a fella who only looks at the center page of *Playboy?* A buff buff?

Did you hear that scream from the corner newsstand? Somebody threw a *Playboy* on top of a *Mademoiselle!*

Is it true that *Playboy* is gonna use a girl from Texas as their Playmate of the Month—just as soon as they can find a page that'll fold out far enough?

What a wonderful sign for a Playboy Club: IF YOU DON'T SEE WHAT YOU WANT—YOU'VE GOT PROBLEMS!

I was going to send *Playboy* a Party Joke, but (politician's name) didn't want to go.

For those of you who have never seen the *Playboy* Calendar—picture a naked *Farmer's Almanac!*

Playmates are what the boys in Vietnam are fighting for—and the boys in Greenwich Village are fighting against!

POLITICIANS

They say one politician got thousands of dollars from testimonial dinners. He's lucky. All I ever get is gas!

Politicians seem to fall into two groups: Those that do their best and those that do their constituents!

It's amazing about some of these politicians. How they can look so straight and be so crooked!

One of these fellas is so crooked, he has to screw his socks on!

I mean, it really shakes you to see one of them sign a piece of legislation—then wipe his fingerprints off the pen!

I know one politician who went to Washington and took the pulse of the nation—and anything else that wasn't nailed down!

A statesman is a politician who didn't get caught.

You can always tell the honest politicians. They're the ones who write thank-you notes!

I'll say one thing for (insert name of politician). He comes up with more surprises than a two-week-old puppy!

They keep talking about one politician as having charisma. Which is a shame. They can cure those things now.

After (insert name of politician's) last few speeches, some of his advisors have suggested he follow the lead of a very famous figure in show business—Marcel Marceau.

It's amazing how many politicians are saying: "I do not choose to run." And nobody's even asking them to walk.

Did you ever get the feeling that (insert name of politician) had greatness thrust upon him—and ducked?

Did you hear about the senator who was a Dove—until one flew over him?

An embarrassing thing happened to (insert name of politician) yesterday. He opened his mouth and a foot fell out.

You might say he has a Windshield Wiper policy on every issue —first one side and then the other!

POLITICS

I just figured out why they call it the New Left. It's so far from being right.

I just had a crazy dream. President Nixon telling a bartender: "My country doesn't understand me!"

Have you heard about that new hurricane they named Hurricane Congress? It's a big wind that goes around in circles.

Congress adjourned. Adjourned—that's what they call it when they go home to goof off—officially.

What this country really needs is Gray Power—thinking!

Do you realize if you took what's happening in Washington today and put it into a situation comedy—the twelve-year-olds wouldn't believe it?

Did you ever get the feeling the only people in Washington who are on their toes are ballet dancers?

The way things are going, the President must feel like the new slacks—permanently pressed!

The President is having the same problem with Congress I have with my wife. Always arguing about money.

I don't know how things are going for The President, but I understand he just had a secret popularity poll taken—and it always will be!

Personally, I think this country is taking a Lassie view of life. We've become obsessed with polls!

A lot of people tend to underestimate the importance of the Vice-President. Let's not forget that he presides over the Senate; functions as the President's special envoy to countries all over the world; and during Cabinet meetings, he's the one who goes out for coffee!

I'm just fascinated by these fellas who get elected governor and then spend all their time traveling. Maybe it's time taxpayers started sending them picture postcards of the state capitol building with the message: WISH YOU WERE HERE!

One governor's been out of the state so long I feel sorry for the people who voted for him. They elected a governor and got an answering service.

I understand they no longer allow cuckoo clocks in Washington —or anything else that tells it like it is.

POLYGAMY

Polygamy is sort of a vague term. Actually, if you have one wife, it's called monogamy. If you have two wives, it's called bigamy. And if you have more than two wives, it's called pigamy!

Believe me, it wasn't easy being a polygamist. Many Mormons used to marry sisters just so they wouldn't have to break in a new mother-in-law!

That's probably why we've never had a Mormon in the White

House. How would it sound—the President saying: "Mr. Ambassador, I'd like to introduce you to the First Lady, and the Second Lady, and the Third Lady, and the—"

POPULATION EXPLOSION

Did you see that headline in this morning's paper? WOMAN EXPECTS 22ND CHILD THIS YEAR! And to think she's still got four months to go!

They say that by the year 2000—we might be growing babies from laboratory cultures. Won't that be a scene? Turning down the lights, putting soft music on the record player, mixing a couple of martinis—then being told by a test tube it's not in the mood?

I can see all kinds of complications. A test tube pointing at a whiskey bottle and yelling: "There he is! That's the father!"

I just figured out why so many fellas in their sixties are becoming fathers. Maybe that Army coffee is finally wearing off!

If you ask me, anyone who becomes a father at sixty isn't paying enough attention to his driving!

With all this talk about automation, no wonder people are having so many babies. It's one of the few things left unskilled labor can produce!

PORNOGRAPHY

The new thing in movies is male nudity. Nowadays the only thing that's being zipped is addresses!

I've seen three movies where the male star appears nude. Now it must be a trend, right? Who could be this forgetful?

And they're always photographed from the back. You don't know if it's an actor or a model for Parker House rolls!

You can't even call this acting. It's more like a personal appearance. Very!

I know one actor who got three jobs like this. One from his resumé and two from his baby pictures!

I know another actor who hasn't worked in three months because of a very rare ailment—diaper rash!

I don't know why they say movies are becoming immoral. Why I just saw one where in the very first reel the hero gets married —so he can join a wife-swapping club!

I can remember when if you wanted to hear cursing, you went to the poolroom. Now you go to the movies.

I saw one picture that's so dirty you get arrested just for reading the marquee.

It's getting so bad, they're running these pictures with English titles. The heavy breathing drowns out the sound track.

I just saw the most sophisticated Western of them all. The hero was wearing a white hat—but it was from Lilly Daché!

POSITIVE THINKING

I believe in mind over matter. Every morning I get up and say: "I'm feeling great! I'm feeling wonderful!" It's called SNOW THYSELF!

Psychology is a fat, homely girl who's crazy about classical music —calling herself a symphomaniac!

Personally, I want to live life to the fullest. I want to avoid probate and nothing else!

If at first you don't succeed—welcome to the club!

People ask me why I'm so ambitious, and I always reply with something a wise old man once said to me: "Beggars can't be boozers!"

We should always keep our temper. Let's face it, there's only one person who encourages us to get our back up—a nurse with a flu shot!

POST OFFICE

Postage is now so high, when they come around for taxes I'm gonna tell them: "I'm sorry. I gave at the Post Office!"

It's ridiculous—ten cents to airmail a letter! It's like I wrote to the Postmaster: "Just fly it. Don't show it movies!"

I can't get over it. Ten cents to air mail a letter! Do you know what a discount Post Office could do in this country?

Just for laughs, why don't we all go down to the Post Office and try to bargain? "Sir, I'd like to airmail this letter for seven cents." "I'm sorry. Airmail is ten cents." "Send it Tourist!"

Do you realize if postage gets any higher, it's gonna be cheaper to go yourself?

Postage is now so high, there's a new respect for anyone who gets a letter. You can tell. Yesterday I got an advertisement addressed to MR. Occupant!

Have you noticed how informal those OCCUPANT mailings are getting? I got one today. It said: "Dear Occ:"

I've got a terrible problem. I'm getting so much mail addressed to Occupant, I've forgotten my name!

I know one fella who put trading stamps on envelopes and it saved him $42 in one year. Who's he gonna write from Leavenworth?

If the Post Office really wants to make money, it's easy. Charge $10 for the greatest status symbol of them all—an unlisted zip code!

Those zip codes are fantastic. I saw one the other day—38-22-36. Which is embarrassing. How do you tell your psychiatrist you're in love with a zip code?

Did you hear about the mailman who had a strange sense of humor? Every time a husband sent his wife a postcard saying: HAVING A WONDERFUL TIME. WISH YOU WERE HERE, he'd erase the last "E".

But you gotta admit the mails are improving. Thanks to airmail, they now get letters from Los Angeles to New York in five hours. Especially the ones to Hawaii.

Isn't it discouraging when it takes two days to fly a letter from coast to coast? I get so mad I mark them AIR-SNAIL!

I won't say the mails are slow, but if Paul Revere had been a letter carrier, we'd now be the Fifty Colonies!

I finally figured out what's wrong with the Post Office. "Neither snow, nor rain, nor heat, nor gloom of night stays these couriers from the swift completion of their appointed rounds." Maybe they've just been getting too many nice days!

It's no good to be too ambitious. Like I knew a postmaster of a branch office who wanted to get ahead in the worst way. So he started holding sales.

POVERTY

We were so poor, you know how some people order half a watermelon? We did it with grapes!

We were so poor, in our family the higher-priced spread was lard!

I really shouldn't complain about my brother-in-law 'cause last year he had a salary that ran to five figures—$469.33.

I won't say what I'm getting paid, but the guy next door cashes my check—and he's on welfare!

We're so poor I'll bet we're the only family on the block with wind-up TV!

You know what's wrong with the world today? We have socks that stretch and budgets that don't!

I was going to put the family on a budget, but I figured if Washington can't manage on one, what chance do we have?

Sometimes I wish the economy would have more bounce and my checks less.

My checks don't exactly bounce. They twitch a little.

I paid my bills, and now I've got the only bank account in town with an echo!

I'm so broke I don't have to avoid probate. Probate avoids me!

I'll say one thing for being poor. It's inexpensive!

I'm so broke, you know how some people have lost confidence in the dollar? I think the dollar has lost confidence in me.

I haven't seen a twenty-dollar bill in so long, I'd have to be introduced to Jackson!

The last paycheck I put in the bank had an NRA sticker on it! . . . I used it as collateral for three dozen apples and a street corner.

I don't wanna complain, but I'm so broke, an orphan in Korea is supporting *me!*

It's amazing. The way they're charging for food, rent, clothing, and taxes—it costs you $300 a week just to be a pauper!

PRICES

Prices are so high it's ridiculous. You go to Tiffany's and they have three things in the window: A diamond tiara, an emerald necklace, and a pork chop!

But it's amazing the way prices are rising. Last month the cost of living went up 45¢ a fifth!

It's really a shame. I've got kids at home who *know* the value of the dollar—and are they discouraged!

You can't believe what's happening to the cost of living. Take orgies. Do you know what they're charging for grapes?

I can remember when a one-armed bandit was a slot machine. Now it's a supermarket cash register!

That's one of the big problems in America today—food prices. Sometimes known as the High Cost of Burping!

Beef prices are so high, even frankfurter makers are finding it hard to make both ends meat.

I didn't realize it myself until my wife sent me in to get an estimate on a veal cutlet.

My wife is trying to save by getting chopped meat and serving it in different ways. On Monday it was hamburger. On Tuesday it was meat loaf. On Wednesday it was tartar. On Thursday it was meat balls. On Friday I couldn't resist. I came into the kitchen and said: "How now, ground cow?"

Doesn't it make you feel a little insecure to know if you're a human being, your body is worth 98¢—and if you're a cow, it's worth $600?

And I've been having a lot of trouble with our butcher. One time I said: "Where did you get that turkey you sold us—from a San Francisco night club?" He said: "Why would I get a turkey from a San Francisco night club?" I said: "Why not? It was topless!"

PRODUCTS

I just saw an interesting statistic. That 94 per cent of American homes have television sets—and only 91 per cent have bathtubs. Which means that more brains are getting washed than anything else!

Everything's speeded up. Remember the little match girl? Today she's pushing Ronson lighters!

Did you ever see one of those electric carving knives work? Looks like a nervous mugger!

I think there's something wrong with my electric toothbrush. It stays still and my arm spins around.

I brought one lifetime pen back after two weeks. I said: "It's a lifetime pen and it just stopped!" They said: "We'll exchange it." I said: "Never mind that. Does it know something?"

I tell you, this world is getting too complicated. Someone just gave me a battery-operated paperweight!

Nowadays everybody knows the troubles we've seen. Home movies!

On top of all the other labor-saving devices, paper clothing will eliminate doing the laundry. Do you realized what this means? If this keeps up, the biggest dust collector around the house will be your wife!

PROTEST SONGS

Have you heard about the latest singing group? Four music lovers who sing protest songs about people who sing protest songs.

I wonder if the President ever feels inadequate, listening to these kids sing their protest songs? Let's face it. Not only do they have the answer to every problem facing the world today—but it rhymes too!

You think it's easy writing these protest songs? What rhymes with Armageddon?

A lot of teen-agers are singing folk songs to protest the war. I can understand how they feel. On the other hand, I'm kinda glad we didn't face the British at Lexington with "Jimmy Crack Corn and I Don't Care!"

PSYCHIATRY

The nicest part about telling your troubles to a bartender—when has a psychiatrist ever given you one on the house?

Did you hear about the psychiatrist who specializes in teen-agers? Instead of a couch, he uses a back seat.

Nowadays we don't treat mental illness by sending people to the madhouse. We charge $35 an hour and send them to the poorhouse!

Psychiatry is when you pay $35 an hour to squeal on yourself!

I know a fella who started off with a personality that was split—and ended up with one that was broke!

Did you ever have one of those awful days—when you go to your psychiatrist and one half of your split personality rats on the other?

Nerve is going to a psychiatrist for a split personality and asking for a group rate!

And psychiatrists today have highly advanced techniques—like giving their patients shock therapy. The bill!

Another new technique is tranquilizers. Little pills you take to keep from being a big one!

Then there's group therapy—the psychiatrist's answer to automation.

Group therapy is where ten people get together to solve their own problems—and at $20 apiece, the psychiatrist's too!

But it's great the way psychiatrists always throw those big words at you. I went to one and he said: "Yes, I see you're suffering from a Cashew-Maraschino Syndrome." I said: "What's that?" He said: "Nutty as a fruit cake!"

Isn't that nice? They just appointed a resident psychiatrist for Yellowstone Park. No couch—sleeping bags!

I had an awful week. Yesterday I went to a psychiatrist and

told him my terrible suspicion. I think my wife is slowly becoming a nymphomaniac. He said: "And you want me to stop it!" I said: "No. I want you to speed it up!"

Psychoanalysis is when you pay $35 an hour to talk to a ceiling.

I know a fella who gave his psychiatrist a birthday present. A slow watch.

I don't mind spending 50 minutes a day on a couch, but for $35 at least I should have company!

I know a psychiatrist who just went bankrupt. People kept giving him a penny for his thoughts!

PUBLISHING

With some publishing houses, it's not unusual for an author to publish and perish.

Personally, I don't mind if a publisher rejects my work. It's when they return it by "junk mail."

I just heard about the greatest book club. You send them $20, and once a month for the next 12 months—they leave you alone!

I don't wanna put down the publishing industry, but they are getting kind of sneaky. I just bought a book *She Lost It at the Palace*. Guess what it was? *Cinderella!*

Another book was called *No Bed of My Own!* Sounds good, huh? *Goldilocks and the Three Bears!*

Do you realize what would happen if Moses were alive today? He'd go up to Mount Sinai, come back with the Ten Commandments, and spend the next eight years trying to get them published!

PURCHASING POWER

I'm really worried about the way the purchasing power of the dollar is falling. Any faster and George Washington gets the bends!

Isn't it frightening the way the value of the dollar is dropping? First it was Monopoly that gave you play money. Now it's the government!

I'll be honest. With all this talk about the devaluation of the dollar, I've got all my money tied up—in fear!

Look on the bright side of things. If the dollar does lose its value, think how good it will make you feel when you send your ex-wife her alimony check!

R

RACE RELATIONS

I've got an uncle who calls himself a consultant on race relations. He's a tout.

Did you hear about the world's most bigoted neighborhood? If you come back from Florida with a tan, they burn a cross on your lawn!

I just met the world's dumbest bigot. He went up to an Indian and said: "Why don't you go back to where you came from?"

I just found out what a honky is. It's someone who blows his car horn a second after the light turns green!

I know a Negro civil rights leader who does so much traveling, it can be confusing and embarrassing too. Like he got in a cab and said: "125th Street in Harlem." And the cab driver refused to take him. My friend said: "Is this discrimination?" The cabbie said: "No. It's Cleveland!"

Remember when the only people promising a long hot summer were resort owners?

Mississippi is a curious mixture of the old and the new. Like, there's a company down there that makes air-conditioned slave quarters!

RADIO

Can you imagine driving along a parkway, listening to the car radio—suddenly the announcer breaks in and says: "We have just received a news flash of such import, that it will affect the future of every man, woman and child on this earth for 300 years to come!" And at this very moment you go under a bridge—and when you come out, an orchestra is playing soft music.

I've always had trouble with car radios. Like the one I've got now is so old, a little white dog keeps coming around to listen to it.

But the thing that bothers me most is the way it fades when we go under things—like clouds, birds, smog—

This radio is so good at fading, it's getting offers from Las Vegas!

Fortunately, the electronics industry is working on the problem, and they've now come up with a radio that's so powerful, it won't even fade going through car washes. It may gargle a little.

Have you listened to some of these talk shows on radio? You don't know if they're trying to bring back conversation or the Stone Age!

The whole idea of these shows is anything goes—and the first thing is manners!

It's amazing. I heard a moderator say to a guest: "I know your type. You're nothing but a sick, phony, crummy creep! And that goes for Dad, too!"

And you can tell one of these moderators is a sadist. There's only one type of guest he's nice to—the masochists!

Listening to these shows, you realize parents have two big problems. Teaching their kids how to behave in polite society—then finding some.

The big theme of these shows are U.F.O.s spotted by U.F.O.s. Unidentified Flying Objects seen by Unbelievably Fuzzy Observers!

And the guests you can't believe! One said he spent the week end on Venus with a moon maiden. The moderator said: "Was it fun?" He said: "No. We couldn't produce luggage!"

RAILROADS

In New Jersey, they're experimenting with a train that goes 170 miles an hour. Which isn't a bad way to go through New Jersey.

One hundred seventy miles an hour and everybody's impressed. I got news. If you're a teen-ager, that's for driveways!

Observers say that even at 170 miles an hour, it's a very quiet train. Of course. Who talks while they're praying?

I understand the railroads are carrying so few passengers, yesterday someone called one up and said: "What time does the next train leave for Boston?" They said: "What time would you like it to?"

Personally, I've always preferred traveling by train. It's roomier; it's more relaxed; and you know the conductor is never gonna sit in the lap of the engineer!

I don't see what railroad workers are complaining about. I was telling my wife that just yesterday I saw three trains with bar cars. She said: "So what? Lots of trains have bar cars." I said: "Freight trains?"

I just read an incredible statistic. One expert says that in 1972, 4 million box cars will get loaded. I didn't even know they drank!

RED CHINA

I wish Red China would stop insulting us. It's getting harder and harder to tell them from an ally.

My wife is a China Watcher. After every meal, I wash the china and she watches.

I've come to one conclusion about the Far East. It isn't far enough.

The big problem with having two Chinas in the U.N. is—who's gonna be in Column A?

People keep arguing about the two Chinas. In my neighborhood, we've always had two Chinas. One for meat and one for dairy!

They say the Chinese are inscrutable. So how come there are 800 million of them?

Do you realize there are 800 million Chinese? . . . 800 million! I know they read the teachings of Mao Tse-tung, but some of them must be sneaking a peek at *Fanny Hill* too!

But they are starting a birth-control program based on bowing. One person joined the program and said: "Bowing? Is that before or after?" The doctor said: "Instead of!"

I don't know why Washington doesn't listen to me. I have a way of neutralizing Red China in just 25 years. It's a combination of rice and the Pill!

I wish they wouldn't talk about accommodating Red China. I mean, I've got a one bedroom apartment!

I'm doing my bit to bridge the gap between China and the United

States. I just invented a new pair of chopsticks. One has a sharp edge and the other has tines.

I used to go with a Chinese girl, but it didn't work out. Every time I bit her ear lobe, two hours later I was hungry again!

In Red China, they're printing the speeches of Mao Tse-tung on underwear. Now every time one of them sits down, he speaks for all of us!

I can't even imagine a civil war in Red China. Who could sing "Dixie" in Chinese? I couldn't even whistle it!

The trouble with Red China is—they're so confused. Like last week a Red Chinese spokesman claimed things were so bad in the United States, we didn't even have enough clothes to put on our backs. And he showed a copy of *Playboy* to prove it!

Did you know there's a kid in Red China who's seven feet tall and weighs 400 pounds? He's the one who delivers those wall newspapers!

I don't wanna say anything about those Chinese wall newspapers, but have you ever tried to wrap a fish in one?

RELIGION

Frankly, I can't believe God is dead—and Forest Lawn didn't get the funeral!

God isn't dead. He's just waiting for us to negotiate.

I wonder what a minister thinks when he walks along something called The Miracle Mile?

I guess you heard about the girl trumpet player who hadda leave the Salvation Army. Her mother didn't want her hanging around street corners.

I know a minister who describes part of his congregation as New Tie—New Suit Christians. They only show up in church on Christmas and Easter!

I wonder how many of those people who abbreviate Christmas—would be content to go to the First Church of X?

You could always tell an atheist during the Crusades. They were the ones who wanted to negotiate.

I've always been fascinated by churches that run bingo games. It's like, out front they ought to have a sign: COME LET US PREY.

I was in a church once that announced its Wednesday night bingo game—then everybody stood up and sang: BRINGING IN THE SHEEP!

You know what's wrong with religion today? There are too many people practising it—and not enough people good at it!

I keep having an awful dream—that one day the meek actually do inherit the earth, and there's no one around to protect us from the Martians.

I don't see why religion and science can't get along with each other. What's wrong with counting our blessings with a computer?

Is it true, if you're a Unitarian, bigots burn a question mark on your lawn?

At this time, we'd like to depart from our usual format to present a gentleman who will give a brief talk on the fantastic progress being made by the ecumenical movement. And here he is—Bishop Ginsberg!

RESORTS

I just heard the saddest story. In Miami Beach they hired an

Eskimo lifeguard but they had to let him go. He kept giving nose-to-nose resuscitation!

Everything is so chic in Miami Beach. Like, where else can you see contact sunglasses?

Hotels are places where fellas who attend conventions rarely observe any.

I know a lot of hotels where chambermaid is a verb!

Personally, I'll never be impressed by people who go over Niagara Falls in a barrel. If they make a round trip—maybe.

I'm just fascinated by Niagara Falls. Like, where else can you find beds with safety belts!

Wouldn't that make a great name for a honeymoon hotel—The Mood? Just think. Thousands of newlyweds sending postcards saying: "I'm in The Mood for love!"

Some of these summer resorts are so sneaky. One has big posters —EARLY AMERICAN ATMOSPHERE. You travel 300 miles to get up there, then you find out what this means—no plumbing!

But it's one of those swingin' resorts. Like, one afternoon they were playing William Tell. This fella was standing there with a wallet on his head—and three girls were trying to hit it with their room keys!

Will Rogers said: "I never met a man I didn't like." And girls coming back from summer resorts make it even shorter: "I never met a man!"

RESTAURANTS

Have you noticed in most restaurants today, the food is frozen and the help is fresh?

Did you hear about the French restaurant that serves a very small dessert? It's a mini-mousse.

Some people have a knack for doing the wrong thing. Like, if he opened a romantic little restaurant with soft lights and wine—he'd have a strolling Gypsy tuba player.

It's a little embarrassing eating in Berkeley. The alphabet soup only comes with four letters.

I proposed to my wife in a restaurant. I had ordered a steak and french fries—and she had ordered pickles and ice cream.

If (name of a very exclusive restaurant) has such great food, how come you don't see more truck drivers eating there?

A true gourmet is someone who knows where to buy a hot knish in Cairo.

I love to eat in Jewish restaurants. Like, where else can you get hot Star-of-David buns?

Now there's a take-out restaurant called The Home. It's for wives who want to give their husbands Home-cooked meals!

I love to look at the pastry they have restaurants keep under those round plastic covers. I think one doughnut was celebrating its second anniversary.

I don't know how old the pies were, but they came in three different flavors—apple, cherry, and dust.

I dig this town. I mean, where else can you find people paying their Diner's Club tab with a welfare check?

RETIREMENT

I dunno. All over the country people are talking about how business is great. I got a friend whose business couldn't be worse. He holds orgies for senior citizens.

Funny thing about it is, it sounded like a great idea. All these people sitting around with nothing to do.

Naturally, some precautions were necessary. All the grapes would have to be seedless.

The nectar wouldn't come from the Gods—from Geritol.

And the wild games would have to be specially designed—like Over 65 Switch. You don't do it with wives—with eyeglasses.

It stands to reason, nobody takes off their clothes at these things. Not because of modesty—because of drafts!

You can't believe what goes on in some of these retirement cities. Ever hear of Strip Shuffleboard?

Retirement is when you spend the afternoon deciding which television shows to watch in the evening, so you'll have something to think about in the morning.

RIOTS

What with mini-skirts and riots, standing on the corner can be pretty exciting!

European boutiques are now selling going-away gifts for people coming to America. It's a combination guidebook and first-aid kit.

Everybody's so nervous. All you gotta do is light a fire for a barbecue and you'll have 42 cops for dinner!

Never before in history has so much merchandise been moved with so few receipts.

Did you hear about the girl who dreamt she went to (riot city) in her Maidenform Bra—and came back with a whole new wardrobe?

You could tell the moderates in (riot city). They were the ones who only took things that were on sale.

They claim it was spontaneous, but it's the first time I ever saw a looter with a shopping list!

I won't say how bad the looting was, but I saw a mannequin practising karate!

This is the only city I know where you can buy Black and Blue Cross.

I haven't seen so much violence since Nasser sang "We Shall Overcome" in Miami Beach!

The average American is someone who deplores violence in the streets and has seen *High Noon* five times.

Remember the good old days—when trouble in the streets meant pot holes?

I tell you, this violence is spreading. Yesterday six people rioted in Berkeley. They were barbers!

What ever happened to the good old days when kids played Spin the Bottle instead of Spin the Government!

I'll tell you how bad things are getting. Yesterday they paroled six convicts, and they didn't wanna go!

It doesn't make sense—like a Molotov cocktail with an olive in it.

S

ST. PATRICK'S DAY

Personally, I make it a point never to argue with an Irishman on St. Patrick's Day. You'd be amazed how many of the Green aren't Jolly, but they are Giants!

And the Irish are always talking about the wee people. The wee people. I don't know if that's a leprechaun or somebody with a kidney problem!

Did you hear about the hip Irishman? He doesn't see fairies. He sees interior decorators!

But the Irish are great talkers. Show me the man who has kissed the Blarney Stone—and I'll show you a fella with a sex problem!

That's what they do over in Ireland—they kiss the Blarney Stone. I know one tourist who got so excited, he attacked a rock!

Do you know that hundreds of years ago the Irish were the first to use Hertz? They say St. Patrick drove the snakes out of Ireland!

Yes, St. Patrick drove the snakes out of Ireland. Now if they could only find the sneak who's driving everybody else out!

I think my wife is Irish. Every time I eat her cooking I turn green!

I know one fella who drinks so much on St. Patrick's Day, they call him the Irish Stew!

SALESMEN

I know a 38-24-36 receptionist who says that she talks to animals —salesmen!

Is he a salesman? He could sell the Venus de Milo a spray deodorant!

I know a fella who's making a fortune in Africa. Sells THINK BIG signs to pygmies!

Is this fella a salesman? You've heard of people who can sell refrigerators to Eskimos? He can sell bath tubs to hippies!

I won't say people are gullible, but you could sell furniture made from orange crates if you gave it the right name—like California Contemporary.

SAN FRANCISCO

The San Francisco earthquake occurred on April 18, 1906. There was fire, panic, pestilence, hunger. You could tell it was serious. Fisherman's Wharf was open only half a day!

People said San Francisco could never be rebuilt—but strong, courageous, forward-thinking citizens cried out: "San Francisco must be rebuilt! If for no other reason than to give the Giants a place to lose in!"

In San Francisco, there's one sure way of knowing when there's an earthquake. Your Jello stands still!

Fortunately, San Francisco now has an Early Warning System for the first signs of another tremor. It's called Topless Waitresses.

Believe me, these topless restaurants will never last. If you've seen two, you've seen them all!

I won't say this town is wild, but where else have you ever seen a topless choir?

SECRETARIES

Did you hear about the 42-26-35 secretary who's an expert touch typist? She has to be. Can't see the keys!

She claims she's a legal secretary. What does that mean—she's over eighteen?

Wouldn't this make a swingin' will? "I, John Doe, being of sound mind—leave my entire estate to my secretary, being of sound body!"

I haven't been so upset since Margaret asked me what I wanted to name the baby. Margaret—that's my secretary.

Show me to the secretary who can remain calm while all others have gone to pieces—and I'll show you a cool aid!

SHOPPING

Have you ever noticed a husband going into a department store— and he wants to buy something like a negligee for his wife, and he's a little embarrassed by it? So he starts off by looking at handkerchiefs.

I think the most nerve-wracking experience a man can go through is buying a flimsy piece of black unmentionable—even if it's for his wife.

What size do you ask for? You're torn between pride and reality.

Salesgirls wind up picturing a Brigitte Bardot with a little bit of Jackie Gleason thrown in.

So you try to describe your wife's figure with your hands. Which, while not very helpful, is good for a few laughs. According to these hand signals, most wives look just like a Coca-Cola bottle.

I don't think it's an accident that the biggest part of the word installment is stall.

Kids are so sophisticated these days. I saw a 5-year-old go up to a store policeman. He said: "Officer?" The cop said: "Yes?" The kid said: "I want to report a lost mother!"

It's an interesting thing when you're standing in front of one of those three-way mirrors in a clothing store. You spend five seconds looking at the suit—and the rest of the time wondering how much weight you've picked up!

Women live for buying. Next month *Playboy* is running a center-page spread just for women. It's a fold-out receipt!

When shopping, I always try to remember that old saying: "*Caveat emptor.*" Which means: "Beware the unfilled cavity!"

But the greatest gimmick of them all is "10¢ OFF!"—and they never say what.

SHOW BUSINESS

I once knew a gorgeous girl—absolutely stunning—who always wanted to be a movie actress, but one small problem kept holding her back. Her measurements were 26-40-26. She looked like an inside-out Racquel Welch. . . . So to tide herself over, she got a job as a teller in a Hollywood bank. Well the very first day a robber comes in, points a gun at her and says: "Stick 'em up!" She ignores him. He says: "Stick 'em up!" She still ignores him. He says:

"Didn't you hear me? I said: 'Stick 'em up!'" She said: "If I could, I'd be in pictures!"

The saddest story I ever heard is about a Hollywood actress who couldn't even get a job by sleeping with the producer—'cause she had insomnia.

Have I told you about my press agent? This is the only man I know who could get the Second Coming on page 4!

Did you hear about the Pennsylvania stripper who calls herself the Gettysburg Undress?

A sadist is someone who goes to a burlesque show; sits in the first row; waits for a stripper to come out—and yawns!

No matter what you do in show business, somebody has done it before. You know how Maurice Chevalier always wears his hat over one eye? Van Gogh started it!

"This man is going to be one of the hottest personalities this year."
"He's that good?"
"No, he smokes in bed!"

That old-time show business really must have been rough. For instance, let's say you were the King's jester. If your option wasn't picked up, your head was!

Original? He has a bad back just from lifting jokes!

Did you hear about the comic who became a hold-up man? And every time he pulls a job he says: "Shtick 'em up!"

Satire is what to do, when you can't do it good.

SMALL TOWNS

I come from one of those tough little Western towns where there's only one red light at the crossroads—and it ain't on a traffic sign!

This town is so wild, they sell Bibles under the counter!

I come from a very small town outside of Boston. This town is so small, we couldn't afford a strangler. We had a nudger!

You know how the big cities have professional call girls? We had to get along with volunteers!

This town is so quiet, the main street goes through a car wash!

But I'll say one thing for the town. Even though it's small, it does try to keep up with the rest of the country. Like this summer it had a race riot. The bookie didn't pay off!

When it comes to politics, it votes conservative. This town is so conservative, in 1968 it didn't even vote for Nixon—King George III!

Last week the P.T.A. sponsored a program of avant-garde music—Bartok and Lawrence Welk.

This is the only town I know where they still show test patterns on TV—at eight o'clock in the evening!

I don't wanna say anything about the Fire Department, but they'd need two trucks to put out someone with a fever!

And we've got one of those automated police departments. I didn't know it myself until I called and said: "Officer, there's a burglar downstairs and he's putting all our silver into a sack!" And the voice on the other end said: "Don't worry about a thing. Just hang up, remain where you are and we'll be right over! Right over! Right over! Right over!"

SMOKING

According to scientists, inhaling the air of any big city is like smoking two packs of cigarettes a day. I can just see the ads of the future: "I breathe Pittsburgh—it satisfies!"

I just figured out a way to really stop people from smoking. Don't tell 'em it's unhealthy. Tell 'em it's fattening!

Isn't that a great idea—putting charcoal in filter tips? Now you can smoke a cigarette and broil your nose at the same time!

You know, I'm always amazed at the way cigar smokers always bite a little bit off. How come they don't buy the right size to start with?

SOUTHEAST ASIA

I'm just fascinated by the politicians who go to Asia; attend three dinners, six receptions, and twelve cocktail parties—and come back foreign policy experts:
"Tell me, sir, what is your impression of Vietnam?"
"Well, the hors d'oeuvres were good."

February and March is the kite-flying season in Southeast Asia. Every time we suggest something, that's what they tell us to do.

The monsoon season is when everything is covered with water. It's like retirement property in Florida.

I know just how the President feels about Vietnam. I tried to get out of a book club once!

SPACE TRAVEL

Did you see those pictures of the moon? They must have the same gardener I have.

It just shows you. On the moon this kind of land is called bleak and desolate. In New Mexico it's called a chance to invest in the future!

I really envy astronauts who can take those walks in space. Ever since they started showing movies in planes, I've wanted to do the same thing myself!

You know what would stop all this moon exploration? If they found out that one of those craters five miles across wasn't a crater —but a belly button!

On Venus, the temperature is 536 degrees and it's called unfit for human habitation. In Washington, D.C., it's called July.

I knew Venus was uninhabited the first time we sent a rocket past it. Nobody asked for foreign aid!

Personally, I believe intelligent life does exist on Mars. And you know why I think it's intelligent? 'Cause it hasn't tried to get here!

They claim this rocket is one of the largest man-made objects in the world. Which is really upsetting a show girl I know. She thinks she is.

SPIES

You know that spy on television who's always using his shoe as a telephone? Well, this morning it happened. He got Athlete's Ear!

Let's face it. One of the greatest secret agents who ever lived was a woman. Mata Hari! Why some of her best work was done under covers.

You know what must be fascinating? Looking over the budget for the CIA. For instance, 200 million dollars is listed under D.A. You say: "What's D.A.?" They say: "Don't Ask!"

SPEED READING

I just found out what a Speed Reader is. That's an atheist in a Christian Science Reading Room.

I think Speed Reading is a wonderful idea. It lets you get through a modern novel before getting sick.

There's only one trouble with a Speed Reader going through the Encyclopedia Britannica. What do you do with the rest of the evening?

Speed Reading is a wonderful invention. Thanks to Speed Reading, you can now read the titles on a foreign movie before the girl gets her clothes back on.

Slow? He'd need Speed Reading just to finish headlines!

SPORTS

The reason women have never done well at bowling—is a basic conflict of motivation. They feel if they knock all the pins down with the first ball, they get cheated out of a second throw.

Trout fishing is the sport where if you're no good at it, your casting smells—and if you are good at it, your refrigerator smells.

Men are creatures who can wait three hours for a fish to bite—but can't wait fifteen minutes for their wives to dress.

Ski-jumping is where you race down a steep hill and fly 300 feet through the air. I don't wanna be a spoil sport, but there's gotta be a better way to meet nurses!

Let's put it this way, if God had meant us to be skiers, He would have given us Blue Cross!

Personally, I don't play golf. I think there's something psychologically wrong about any game in which the person who gets to hit the ball the most is the loser.

I'll never forget the first time I saw a mini-skirt on a golf course. I was making this 2-foot putt—and missed!

Is it true that it's illegal for Lew Alcindor to fall down unless someone yells: "Timberr!"

I gotta admit, I'm no athlete. To me, an outdoor sport is necking in a convertible!

SPRING

This is the time of year when you get spring fever and yawn a lot—even when you're not watching reruns.

I just heard the first robin of spring chirping. You'd chirp too if you were under 6 feet of snow!

Here it is spring—the time when the Mama Bear says to the Papa Bear: "Wake up. It's half-past April!"

Isn't that a lovely thought? April showers bring May crab grass!

STOCK MARKET

I admit it. I'm a Wall Street fanatic. Like if the world was coming to an end on Friday, the first thing I'd do is sell short!

The big thing today is investment clubs. For the uninitiated—an investment club is a way to lose money by parliamentary procedure.

An investment club is not for plungers. It's more for waders.

Every month you sink $10 into a stock chosen because the son-in-law of the uncle of a fella who is the accountant for the man who takes out the garbage of this company—knows something. . . . What he knows is never to put $10 of his own money into this company!

Investment clubs are known for the fantastic amount of research that goes into their decisions. They discuss price-earning ratios, market trends, stock-splits, capitalization, and can the broker win carrying 145 pounds?

But investment clubs are very valuable to the economy 'cause they don't panic during crashes. They panic during booms— 'cause that's when the treasurer disappears.

Did you hear about the teen-age investment club? They never trust stocks over 30!

They say Wall Street has nothing in common with Las Vegas. So how come my broker just put in a lounge show?

You might be interested in that new mutual fund that stresses growth through prudent, conservative, mature investment. They bet favorites for show.

Conglomerates are nothing new. They used to be called babies.

If you really want to upset a girl, invite her up to your apartment, turn down the lights, put soft music on the record player, pour champagne for two, sit beside her on the couch, take her hand, and in a voice throbbing with emotion—try to sell her a mutual fund!

I'm in one of those go-go funds that try to make a quick profit by jumping in and out of stocks. It's like Group Russian Roulette.

I'm one of those investors who run scared. Like, if I had bought Manhattan Island for $24—two weeks later I would have sold it for $28.

I subscribe to one of those stock-market advisory services. That's a tout with a mimeograph.

I'll say one thing for the stock market. It's healthy. You go down to your broker's office and it's just like a sauna. Everybody's sweating!

And you know what bothers me? When you buy, the broker makes a profit—and if you panic and sell, the broker makes a profit. My broker has only one problem: How to look sad with a smile on his face!

I've got a wonderful broker. I call him Mark. That's short for Marquis de Sade.

They say: "You can't take it with you!—but I dunno. I understand Merrill Lynch just opened an office at Forest Lawn!

I wanna tell you about my broker. You can't believe the things this man has put me into—the poorhouse, analysis, bankruptcy!

What this country needs is a really safe place to put your money. Like a mattress with a growth potential.

I can remember when bonds were called Senior Securities. Now they're more like Senile Securities.

I just heard of a great diet. You only eat when the stock market goes up!

STOCK MARKET—ADVANCING

When it comes to investing, there are certain industries you can't go wrong with. Automobiles in Detroit; steel in Pittsburgh; and prune juice in Sun City!

I don't wanna say anything about my broker, but he should only have sticking into him all the points I.B.M. has gone up since he told me to sell!

Thanks to this man I've gone from Over-the-Counter to Over-the-Barrel.

Fortunately, I'm in something now that's gonna make me a mint! Low-cal birth-control pills for fat swingers!

Have you seen what's going on in the stock market? Nowadays a penny saved is $3.00 lost!

He who hesitates—buys the stock two points higher!

I'd just like to know if the stock market is at a historical high or a hysterical high.

STOCK MARKET—DECLINING

The stock market's going down like a lazy hummingbird!

Nowadays a conservative is anyone who takes his money out of the stock market to go to Las Vegas!

The Optimist on Wall Street is saying: "Wait for the summer rally!" The Pessimist is saying: "What wait? This is it!"

And you can always tell the investors who are sore losers. They're the ones who call it the Dam-Jones Average!

The only way you can really describe the last few weeks in the stock market is with a four-letter word—THUD!

They say it's only a correction, and that's right. What it's correcting is the idea that you can make money in the stock market!

I haven't seen anything go down so fast since Jack E. Leonard got into an elevator!

It's like 1929 on the installment plan. . . . Even my blue chips are turning green!

It's ridiculous. The country has never been more prosperous, and the stock market is plunging. This is gonna be the first depression in history where they'll sell caviar on street corners!

Ant there won't be one breadline—three breadlines! White, rye, and dietetic!

They say that most of the leading economic indicators are pointing down. Which is a problem. How do you feed an economy oysters?

I wish they wouldn't talk about a recession. I still owe $12,000 from the boom!

RECESSION: when you lose your job.
DEPRESSION: when I lose my job.

If you think the stock market is depressed, you oughta see some of the investors who are in it.

You can always tell an investor these days. He's someone who's alert, informed, attuned to the economic heartbeat of America! And he cries a lot too!

I won't say how I've done in the stock market, but you know how some stocks split? Mine just crumble!

My stocks are doing so badly, I even worry on week ends!

You're looking at a fella who left his heart in San Francisco—and everything else on Wall Street.

The main thing is—don't panic! Like I just called my broker. You shoulda heard what I called my broker!

One day I called up my broker and he said: "The market is down thirteen points!" I said: "Thirteen? That's terrible!" He said: "This is no time to get superstitious!"

And you can tell the brokers are worried. One day the Dow Jones was unchanged and they called it a rally!

Fortunately, I haven't been too hurt by the decline. About six months ago I took the Mickey Rooney approach to the market. I went short!

Playing the stock market is like watching the hemline on mini-skirts. You never know when it's gonna touch bottom!

STRIKES

Thanks to this strike, (insert name of company) is getting a lot of sympathy from mothers. They're the only ones who know what it is to have labor pains for two months!

I think it's terrible, all these teachers walking out. It's confusing to the kids. Who are they gonna hit?

I'm not saying there's violence in the schools, but I can understand why teachers turned down a $1050 raise. They spend more than this on Band-Aids!

And do you realize what this strike is doing to the educational gap? We're now two weeks behind the Russians in Sandpile!

I don't know why school teachers want more money. Who do they think they are—TV repairmen?

Frankly, I didn't realize how little money teachers were getting until I saw one buy a Hershey Bar on time!

And if the teachers have any class, when they do go back they'll bring a note from their mothers!

What do you call it when a school teacher takes time off to strike? A Sabatogical?

Between vacations, holidays, and strikes—I know a kid who just graduated from high school and he's never been there! . . . He graduated magna cum seldom!

Think what would have happened if there were teacher strikes in Shakespeare's time. Hamlet, turning to the audience and saying: "To be—or ain't to be!"

I know a kid who has a terrible problem. He's been in this classroom with his hand raised for five hours—and there's nobody to give him permission!

And the parents are really in the middle. They don't know which is worse—having their taxes go up or their kids stay home!

Did you hear about the baking school teachers who went out on strike—for shorter hours and more bread?

SUBURBIA

Have you ever noticed the way a neighbor will stand talking at the front door for 35 minutes, 'cause she doesn't have enough time to come in?

You know what's made barbecuing so popular today? That fluid they use to get the coals started. I'll bet if Nero had had that fluid, he'd have gotten Naples too!

Do you realize this whole country has become hooked on charcoal? It's unbelievable. I know a guy who charcoal broils leftovers!

You go to museums and see pictures of hairy, grizzled men cooking meat outside their shelters. Ten thousand years of progress and what do you see any Saturday or Sunday afternoon? Hairy, unshaven men cooking meat outside their shelters!

SUMMER

Considering the smog, the tornadoes, the rain and the heat—do you really think this Daylight is worth Saving?

Hurricanes make a lot of noise; they do a lot of damage; and man hasn't found a way to control them. No wonder they're named after women!

There's only one sensible way to cope with this weather. Sleep for 22 hours and then, in the afternoon, take a 2-hour nap!

Summertime—and the living is easy. Tell that to a fella who makes ear muffs!

June is when the reruns begin on TV. You know what a rerun is. That's what happens on your *second* day in Mexico.

People with bad memories used to be pitied, up until the time TV started summer reruns.

July and August are when baby-sitters charge 50¢ more an hour 'cause the TV shows are all reruns.

I know a fella who had a terrible accident last summer. He was bitten by a wasp. A white, Anglo-Saxon, Protestant nymphomaniac!

Remember the way summers used to be—when girls were half cotton and half starch?

As Confucius once said: "Man who has air-conditioner repossessed—lose his cool!"

August is when June graduates evaluate the job they got in July—and decide they'll go back for post-graduate work in September.

SUPERMARKET

Did you hear about the little neighborhood grocery store who—every time there's trouble—goes into a phone booth, tears off its walls, and comes out—Supermarket!

SHELF CONTROL: when you go into a supermarket to buy a quart of milk—and all you buy is a quart of milk!

Isn't it amazing what they sell these days in supermarkets? Yesterday I heard a woman ask if the transistor radios were ripe!

I'm so unlucky, I almost walked through a door at the supermarket. The electric eye was nearsighted!

SUPERMARKET CHEATS

I think it's time we considered the greatest credibility gap of them all—comparing the cash-register tape against your supermarket purchases!

I wouldn't say I've been overcharged. Let's just say the checker who rings up sales has a finger that stutters!

Sometimes I think I'd have to win the grand prize in their contests just to get even!

Maybe I'm overly suspicious, but how come the checker always rings up prices as the box boy asks you about your new shoes?

Do you know who the newest public enemy in America is? The housewife! It's amazing what some women have been doing to cheat supermarkets—like hiding small packages in large packages. Last week a woman went to a checkout counter with a 38-pound bag of potato chips! . . . Got 55 Green Stamps and a hernia!

And you can't even blame them for doing this 'cause it's a habit pattern. Women have been hiding small packages in large packages for years—under a different name—falsies!

And there are all kinds of cheating. Like they change the prices. I saw one woman go up to a checkout counter with a 25¢ seven-pound steak. . . . The clerk didn't say a word. Just added an $8.00 shaker of salt.

And how many candy bars have been eaten between the candy counter and the checkout counter? . . . I know one family who's gained 23 pounds without ever getting a receipt!

I won't say how much they eat, but the checkout clerks don't give them Green Stamps—toothpicks!

SUPERMARKET GAMES

I'm just fascinated by the games you play in supermarkets. And if you don't think supermarkets play games, just look at their prices!

I was telling my wife: "You shouldn't go in those stores that have games of chance. They just increase the price on everything else." She said: "That's ridiculous. Now finish your ten-dollar steak!"

Supermarkets now give away so many gifts and prizes and jackpots—the only one who loses is everybody.

I was talking to this fella in a supermarket and he said: "I don't think we're overdoing these games of chance." I said: "Oh? Are you the manager?" He said: "No. The Pit Boss!"

One supermarket is running a real great contest. If you win, they give you the name of a cheaper supermarket!

SUPERMARKET PRICES

The Government is investigating high food prices in supermarkets. I think Washington resents anybody getting our money before it does!

But the thing about supermarkets I can never understand—they sell bottled water for a dollar a gallon—and apple cider for only 79¢ a gallon! Yesterday, Jack Benny came staggering in from the desert and he was saying: (PARCHED VOICE) "Cider! Cider!"

The way they're charging, they ought to be called supermarkups!

I went up to one checkout counter and said to the clerk: "Pardon me, miss, but what's that?" And I pointed. She said: "That's my mouth!" I said: "Thank Heavens! Everything's so high in here, I thought it might be your belly button!"

SURFING

Frustration is a surfer in the Trevi Fountain!

I know a lot of people are worried by what's going on in Asia—but I happen to know our West Coast will never be invaded by the Communists. They'd never get through the surfboards.

I just met the world's richest kid. Has a surfboard that sleeps six!

I know one surfer who makes runs you can't believe. Like he owns the only board in town with curb feelers!

Surfing is almost like a religion to kids. You can tell. They even do it kneeling.

SWIMMING POOLS

Back-yard pools are the new American status symbol. It's the outdoor version of color TV.

Now, for the first time, millions of Americans are able to drown in the privacy of their own home!

I don't even mind drowning so much. It's the idea of climbing up to do it!

My cousin's got a 15,000-gallon pool, and he doesn't put chemicals in—Kool-Aid! . . . Can you imagine going down for the third time in Raspberry?

But it's a sure-fire way to meet the neighbors. The minute you put in a pool, people from miles around are saying: "Have towel, will travel!"

You're not a host anymore—you're a beach boy!

And the kids. They're the worst of all. I won't say what they do—but last year I put 15,000 gallons into the pool—and took 16,000 out!

Do you realize if at this very moment, every back-yard pool in America sprang a leak, we'd all be standing ankle-deep in water?

Can you imagine going home with chlorinated socks?

I got a great idea. Chlorine deodorant for families who want their neighbors to think they own a pool!

T

TARZAN

You remember Tarzan. The fella who's always running around in the leather jockey shorts? . . . Why do you think he has that awful yell? (GIVE TARZAN CALL) They're two sizes two small!

In the original book, Tarzan was a literate, soft-spoken, everyday sort of fella who talked to animals. I know a lot of people talk to animals, but Tarzan waited for an answer.

I was always a little suspicious of Tarzan's span of concentration. Like, in one picture he said: "Me, Tarzan. You, Jane." And she said: "You, Tarzan?" And he said: "Who?"

Isn't that a wonderful name—Cheetah? That's what my wife calls me when I come in at three o'clock in the morning.

TEACHING METHODS

I'd like to say a few words about one of the most popular concepts in modern education—Show and Tell. Show and Tell is a device created by grammar schools to communicate family secrets to 32 other families before 9:15 in the morning!

You don't know what fear is until you've seen your six-year-old leaving for school with a picture of Mother when she was a stripper at Minsky's.

You should hear some of these Show and Tell sessions. The teacher points at a little kid and says:
"And what do you have there, John?"

"I have eighteen thousand dollars in cash."
"And where did you find the eighteen thousand dollars in cash?"
"Under the rug. My father's a doctor!"

Another kid brought in a postcard from his teen-age sister who made a rather hurried trip to Tiajuana. It was a Special Delivery.

If this keeps up, Show and Tell could be the Fanny Hill of the finger-painting set!

The whole gimmick is never to let your kids bring anything valuable to school—'cause three out of four times it's Show and Lose!

Say, I got a great idea. If kids are so wild about Show and Tell— why don't we extend it to homework?

You know one of the drawbacks of the "look-say" method of teaching reading? Every time the kid sees a typographical error, he thinks it's a new word. . . . And when it comes to abbreviations, forget it!

Look-say is learning by pictures—and if you don't think you can learn by pictures, you've never seen *PLAYBOY*.

Look-say has one big advantage. Once again you can leave sexy books around the house and not worry about the kids reading them. . . . At least until they get their Master's. . . . Like *A House Is Not a Home*. Try puzzling that one out with look-say!

Russia is probably the only country in the world that doesn't use the look-say method. For obvious reasons. In Russia you may look—but you don't dare say!

I won't say how the look-say method has worked out, but on college campuses all over the country, Remedial Reading is now more popular than necking!

Have you seen some of the new college textbooks? *Goldilocks and the Three Bears?* . . . Reading time: 14 hours?

They did the only thing they could with Shakespeare. Simplified it: WHO IS THIS? HIS NAME IS HAMLET. HAMLET LIVES IN A BIG HOUSE WITH HIS MAMA. WHERE IS DADA? DADA IS IN FOREST LAWN!

Patience is someone teaching "supercalifragilisticexpialidocious" by look-say.

Now there's a campaign to make the New Math even harder. They want to teach it by look-say!

TEEN-AGERS

Teen-age is a very emotional period—easy glum, easy glow!

There are now one billion teen-agers in this world. Now you know why our Father art in Heaven!

Have you ever gone into a teen-ager's room? They're all done in a very interesting style—Early Slob!

They say all the new TV programing is being aimed at teen-agers. I didn't believe it until they started spreading the rumor that Ed Sullivan has acne!

If television really wants to fascinate teen-agers, it's simple. Take the picture tube out and put a mirror in!

But I'll say this. There's one good thing about having teen-agers. Your bathroom mirror will never be stolen!

I know a father who's having a lot of trouble with his teen-ager. In fact, yesterday he had a man-to-it talk with him.

They say a teen-ager brings sunshine to a house, and that's right. By the time they come home, it's morning!

You know the most dangerous thing a teen-ager can have? A skate-board with a back seat!

Kids were a lot better off when they had more discipline—when the only teeny-boppers were parents!

I think it's wonderful what all these teen-agers have accomplished by joining the Peace Corps. You don't know what a thrill it is to see two primitive African tribes—drag-racing elephants!

What makes kids so awkward? I've got a teen-ager—I think he takes Clumsy Lessons from Humpty-Dumpty!

Kids today are all trying to find themselves. And some of them haven't taken a bath in so long—that shouldn't be too hard!

All teen-agers seem to talk about is getting turned on. Parents today don't know if they've raised a kid or a night light!

Remember when teen-agers were told to visit their dentist at least twice a year? Now it's their parents!

I just saw an interesting letter in one of those advice columns. It said: "We have a sixteen-year-old daughter who doesn't drink, smoke, use drugs, or stay out late. She isn't pregnant and she's a straight A student. Tell me—where did we go right?"

TEEN-AGE APPEARANCE

Did you hear about the teen-ager who spent two years trying to find himself? Got a haircut, and there he was!

One kid was wearing his hair so long, people thought he was Prince Valiant. All night long they kept saying: "Here, Prince! Here, Prince!"

Have you ever heard a teen-ager talking to his barber? "Take a little off around the hips!"

Do you realize if boys look any more like girls—and girls look any more like boys—the only way they're gonna be able to tell the difference is to get married?

Teen-age togetherness is her hair curlers getting caught in his hair curlers.

I finally figured out a way to get teen-agers behind our foreign policy. Create a world-wide shortage of combs and blame it on the Communists!

I know a kid who told me he spends 6 hours a day combing his hair. I said: "Six hours? Why not 8 hours?" He said: "That'd be silly!"

Can you imagine combing your hair for 6 hours a day? When he says something is groovy, it's his scalp!

One fella had hair so long, it kept getting caught in things. Like his toes!

I can't understand this teen-age slogan: NEVER TRUST ANYONE OVER 30. I mean, its all right to like skinny girls, but this is ridiculous!

Teen-agers are even wearing very low-cut gowns. Like Friday, I went to a coming-out party and half of them were!

TEEN-AGE MARRIAGES

You can always tell the parents at a teen-age wedding. They're not throwing rice. They're throwing fits!

You know what's wrong with marriages today? People are promising to love, honor, and obey for ever and ever—who can't even sit through two-hour movies!

Have you noticed, when two kids get married the only one who lives happily ever after is the marriage counselor?

You know what'd straighten out some of these hoods on the motorcycles? Marriage! I can see them now, washing the dishes in their black-leather aprons!

So many young couples are getting married, Niagara Falls now has three separate hotels that cater to teen-agers. To make them feel at home, the rooms don't have beds—back seats!

The problem with all these teen-age marriages is, they don't last long. One teen-age marriage broke up so fast, they were fighting over who gets custody of the acne!

But it's easy to tell a teen-age wedding. The people don't throw rice. They throw Tootsie-Rolls!

Wedding presents are a problem for teen-agers. What do you give to the couple who has nothing? . . . Have you ever been to a shower for a teen-age bride? Instead of 15 toasters, they get 22 Barbie Dolls!

'Course, one of the problems with teen-age marriages is they're a little late. By the time he's popping the question, she's popping a little too!

TEEN-AGE MUSIC

Believe me, it isn't easy writing songs today. What rhymes with screams?

Be honest now. Can you understand the words to these songs? I heard one yesterday. I think it was labor pains with a beat!

I went to one of these teen-age night clubs and the guitars were twanging and the drums were banging and the singers were howling and the dancers were stomping. And I asked a fella with hair down to his shoulders why he wore it that way. He said: "Eh?" I said: "Your hair. Why do you wear it so long?" He said: "What?" I said: "Never mind. I think I know!"

I just heard the saddest story. About a kid who's in love with something that's 40–22–36. The amplifier for his guitar!

TELEPHONE

I won't say my wife gossips, but at our house opportunity has to knock. If it phoned, it'd get a busy signal.

You see the most interesting things written in phone booths. Like: "For really fast, fast, fast relief—call (phone number)."

If you want to lose a teen-ager for weeks, it's simple. Put a phone in the bathroom!

You know the most frustrated person in the world? It's a bookie with one phone and a teen-age daughter!

I know a fella who makes chicken obscene phone calls. Says the most awful things to the Weather Report.

I just heard a crazy phone conversation: "Hello? Is this Sam's Delicatessen? Do you deliver? Good! The pains are coming three minutes apart!"

You know what's nice about all those recorded phone messages? You can finally tell the operator what she can do with her advice.

I won't say how much wire-tapping is going on, but they asked a politician: "Do you do much public speaking?" He said: "Yes. I have a private phone in Washington!"

Personally, I blame the phone company. If they're gonna let all these people listen in, the least they could do is charge you for a party line!

I don't wanna brag, but there are so many people listening in to my phone, every time I dial I get stage fright!

Then there's the telephone service for atheists. You dial a number and somebody crosses their fingers for you!

TELEVISION

Remember the good old days when TV was something in the future, rather than in the living room?

I discovered television was in trouble when a twelve-year-old got up and shut it off—after a ten-year-old asked him to.

I've been watching television for 15 years now—on and off. And that's the way I prefer it—off!

Last week, I saw one show that was so bad, I went out to the kitchen for leftovers!

And I get very upset by the news on television. Like yesterday I put my foot through Walter Cronkite!

I know a fella who lives beside a nudist camp and it's so embarrassing. TV rating services keep calling him up to ask him what he's watching.

I won't say what my wife does all day, but you can fry eggs on our picture tube!

According to a recent poll, the more intelligent a person is, the less he watches television. Personally, I think they have it backwards. The more a person watches television, the less intelligent he becomes!

Anyone who thinks Pay TV is something new—has never called in a repairman!

You know what upsets me? Color TV! Especially when it's out of adjustment—which is always. . . . I turned it on last night and it was awful. I didn't know if the set needed tuning or the picture tube threw up!

I don't mind telling you, I'm worried. This year there was no second season on television. Do you think the networks gave up on us?

TELEVISION COMMERCIALS

You know what I like about watching television? The commercials! According to them the biggest problem facing America today is bad breath!

I just heard a sad story. About a fella who's so impressed by that bad-breath commercial on TV, every time he goes into a drug store to buy the product—he's afraid to open his mouth!

Did you hear about the 300-pound secretary whose boss wouldn't take her to lunch because she has bad breadth!

What's the big problem? It's easy to tell if you have bad breath. People treat you like royalty. They back away!

And have you noticed how good the commercials are getting? I saw a commercial that was so good, at the end it had credits!

Let's face it. There are some things in this world you can count on. Like, you will never see a commercial with an unhappy ending!

You know the commercial that always shakes me? The one about rough, red hands. Makes you sound like a Communist dishwasher!

Believe me, there's nothing wrong with rough, red hands. If you've got an itch, there's so much more to scratch with!

TV commercials are those few brief moments when you pay attention to your wife and kidneys.

You know what upsets me? The way they turn up the volume on commercials. Commercials are now so loud, if you go to the bathroom during one—it comes right in with you!

Isn't it upsetting when you watch a movie on television you've already seen—and the only thing that looks familiar is the commercials?

It's fascinating the way every ten minutes they break up these movies with commercials. I saw the story of Lindbergh, and I still don't know if he flew over the Atlantic or Katy Winters!

TELEVISION—DAYTIME SERIALS

I was talking to my wife yesterday afternoon. I didn't say much. How much can you say between "Edge of Night" and the "Secret Storm"?

I believe in things that endure—a mother's love; the beauties of nature; the plots on daytime TV!

Have you noticed how every daytime serial has a character called the black sheep of the family? The black sheep of the family. I think the networks have a ranch out in Montana growing them!

And this nogoodnik is always doing mean things—like embezzling the family fortune; foreclosing Widder Brown's mortgage; going down to old Doc Simpson's drugstore and mixing aspirins with the birth-control pills!

I know an actor who was a villain on one of these shows and it was just fantastic. He'd go in a supermarket and strange women would hit him with umbrellas! . . . It was like being Resident Egyptian in Miami Beach!

You know what gets me? The way they claim these stories are

all true to life. When have you ever had a crisis that was interrupted by a commercial?

TELEVISION PROGRAMS

I just had a horrible dream. The President goes on television and declares that on reliable scientific authority he has been advised that the world will come to an end at midnight—and nobody hears it 'cause they're running a movie against him!

It's amazing how many movies are being (popular TV show) shown on TV. Why I just met a fella who's the star of his own show. I said: "You're an actor?" He said: "No. A projectionist!"

I've seen so many movies for the second time—it's like, every night, two hours of my life is on reruns!

I think it's fascinating the way they cut up pictures for television. Any day now we're going to be seeing *Cleopatra* as a short!

I just saw a movie on TV that was so old, France was on our side!

I tell you, TV is going too far. Now they're running a soap opera with a sob track!

TV critics are calling this the Citrus Season. One lemon after another!

Overkill is a funny little thought made into a half-hour situation comedy.

I won't say anything about the new comedy shows, but it's the first time I ever saw a laugh track throw up!

One TV show is so bad, the studio monitors are tuned to another channel!

Another show was canceled so fast all you could hear was the laugh track saying: "Where'd everybody go?"

I keep having this terrible nightmare. That all 1100 Nielsen families go away on vacation at the same time—and everybody gets canceled!

TEXAS

It's one of those typical Texas homes. Even the kitchen has seven rooms.

I just had an unusual experience. Met this fella, 6 feet tall, wearing a 10-gallon hat, cowboy boots, lots of money, owns oil wells and a cattle ranch. What makes it so unusual, he's from Vermont.

There's one town in Texas that has so much money even the Volkswagens are Cadillacs!

Did you hear about the Texan who's so rich, he has the Sunday *Times* sent airmail?

I know a fella from Texas who's so rich he just had his gums capped!

Is it true in Texas they tell rich orthodontist jokes?

I don't care how much money you have—if you want to feel poor, go to a picnic in Texas. Even the paper plates are sterling!

THANKSGIVING

The Russians put out a news report that things are so bad in this country that on November 24th a hundred million Americans will be eating stale scraps of bread. And they will be—stuffing!

Having the relatives over on Thanksgiving eliminates one big problem—leftovers. They've been coming over for ten years now, and the only thing we've had to get rid of is them!

But on Thanksgiving I try to be thankful for the little things. Like, if my lifetime pen lasts six months.

And just before eating Thanksgiving dinner, there's something else we can be thankful for. That turkeys don't have the Pill!

Everybody was thankful at the first Thanksgiving. The Pilgrims were thankful they had landed safely in the New World—and the Indians were thankful they hadn't landed 200 years earlier!

Frankly, if I had been an Indian—I'd have wished Plymouth Rock had landed on the Pilgrims!

And the Indians weren't too happy about the Pilgrims moving next door. In the history books, they might have been Pilgrims—but to the Indians, they were blockbusters!

The Indians weren't prejudiced. They just knew what happened to real estate values when white people moved in. Take Manhattan Island. Nice place? Hadda let it go for $24!

Incidentally, the history books are wrong about one thing. They claim the turkey the Pilgrims roasted on that first Thanksgiving was wild. This is only half true. He was not wild—until he found out what they had in mind!

Nowadays all you can buy is frozen turkeys. Turkeys are so frozen, that for the first three hours in the oven they're enjoying it!

After one Thanksgiving I asked my wife: "Is this a frozen turkey?" She said: "Yes." I said: "My compliments to the refrigerator!"

I wanna tell you what kind of a cook my wife is. When she takes that turkey out of the oven and removes the aluminum foil —she's throwing away the best part!

One year the turkey was unbelievable. I said: "Where did you get this recipe?" She said: "It's a very good recipe. I got it out of a magazine!" I said: "Which one? *Popular Mechanics?*"

Do you realize what they're getting for turkeys? Sixty-nine cents a pound! The main thing we should be thankful for is the Pilgrims didn't celebrate with steak!

TOPLESS

I know a sixty-year-old fella who's very unimpressed with these topless dancers. He says: "Not only does my wife have everything these young kids have—but it's at counter level!"

I just saw the craziest thing. A topless restaurant with a sign saying: WATCH YOUR HAT AND COAT!

Did you hear about the topless club that went out of business? There was only one thing flatter than their drinks—their waitresses.

Skinny? You'd need three of her to make one topless waitress!

If topless gets any more popular, they're gonna be selling bras with instructions!

Personally, I've got nothing against topless waitresses—darn it!

I even have a topless contract with my agent. Everything I earn, he takes 10% off the top.

Topless isn't new. Why topless was mentioned hundreds of years ago in a nursery rhyme: "One for the money, two for the show!"

Did you hear about that new insurance policy that protects you against topless waitresses? It's called Double Indemnity!

TOURISTS

Thanks to modern jet air travel, now we can be sick in countries we never even heard of before.

Did you ever get the impression that to qualify as a tourist paradise, some of these countries are importing their water from Mexico?

Last year I took one of those Dysentery Tours—14 bathrooms in 7 days!

They even made a movie about it—*The Loneliness of the Short-Distance Runner.*

Someone asked me: "Did you see the fountains of Rome?" I said: "If it flushed, I saw it!"

Really. If any of you are going to Europe, I gotta give you my recipe for the perfect martini. Three parts gin to one part Kaopectate!

My big problem was the tour guide. Every day we stopped in 22 souvenir shops and 1 rest room. Naturally. Who gets kickbacks from rest rooms?

And tour guides are very big for tips. These are the only people who can clear their throats in 15 different languages!

As a side trip we went to Africa, and you oughta see the things I brought back with me. How do you spell malaria?

Customs examiners are the only men I know who don't get excited by a 42-26-38 figure. Too often, the 42 is watches.

We had a pretty easy time going through Customs. The inspector asked my wife to open her suitcase, pulled out a negligee, put it on, skipped away, and we never saw him again!

Remember the good old days—when people who couldn't afford to go to Europe, didn't?

U

UNIONS

Can you imagine the whole world being created in 6 days and 6 nights? Fortunately, now we have unions!

If the unions were smart, they wouldn't tie salaries up to the Cost of Living but to the National Debt.

I won't say the auto workers' settlement was inflationary, but next year we might be paying $5000—and that's a lot of money for windshield wipers!

Did you hear about the auto worker who was offered a job as bank president—but he couldn't take the cut in salary?

An auto worker is someone who gets a dollar an hour raise and wants to know why a loaf of bread costs 48¢.

You know what really hurts? I know a Ford worker who got such a big increase, he can finally afford a Cadillac!

UNITED NATIONS

You meet such fascinating people at the U.N. One fella had on a purple uniform, gold epaulettes, a green hat with orange plumes, and sequinned spats. I said: "I dig that uniform. What are you in?" He said: "The Secret Service!"

I visited the U.N. and a Russian was saying: "The United States is a militaristic nation. Why one of the most popular TV shows in the country is headed by the military!" I said: "One of the most popular TV shows in America is headed by the military? What show is that?" He said: "Captain Kangaroo!"

The U.N. could be the world's first Teflon-coated organization. Nothing they do ever seems to stick.

V

VACATION

There's only one problem when you go away for a vacation. You can turn off the gas. You can turn off the electricity. But you can't turn off the rent!

A vacation is when you take two weeks off from work—and then spend the next few months trying to put them back!

As you travel around the country, it's amazing how many signs you see: GEORGE WASHINGTON SLEPT HERE! GEORGE WASHINGTON SLEPT HERE! GEORGE WASHINGTON SLEPT HERE! I figure the revolution could have been two years shorter if George had known about No Doz!

Nowadays a voice crying in the wilderness isn't a prophet—it's a tourist whose wife read the map!

There's something about every vacation you never forget. In my case it was an embroidered sampler on the wall of the Hall of Mirrors in Versailles. It said: BE IT EVER SO HUMBLE, THERE'S NO PLACE LIKE HOME.

W

WAR SCARES

Bomb shelters are a lot like short skirts. Every few years they come back in style again.

I didn't realize how uptight everything is until I ordered Russian dressing in a restaurant—and the CIA took a picture of me on the way out!

I'll tell you how bad things are in Washington. The Hot Line is no longer to Moscow—it's to Dial-a-Prayer!

It doesn't make sense. Like an answering service for the Hot Line!

WATER POLLUTION

Remember the good old days—when water pollution was a Saturday night bath?

I asked the Water Commissioner: "Is our water pure?" He said: "As pure as the girl of your dreams!" So I switched to root beer!

It's not that the (name of river) water isn't fit to drink—but where else can you see fish coughing?

I'll tell you how bad water pollution is getting. Half the scuba diving equipment sold in this country today is going to fish!

WIFE

I'm getting a little suspicious of my wife. She said that ten times as many people drown in bathtubs as do in swimming pools. So yesterday I came home and there was a lifeguard in her bathtub!

For years my wife has talked about having a catered affair and frankly, I never paid much attention till yesterday—when I found her in bed with the delicatessen man.

My wife has a rather peculiar turn of mind. Like, last month she sent away $150 for one of those courses that builds men. All right —but last week alone she built three of them!

Nerve? Every time we eat in a restaurant, she asks for a bag to take things home—steak, cutlery, napkins. . . . I've seen vacuum cleaners that don't scoop up as much!

I don't wanna say she's cheap, but she's got a Kleenex in her pocketbook that's three years old! . . . the lint it leaves is gray!

I won't say what my wife does all day, but she just had something removed from her back—a mattress!

I never knew my wife was nearsighted until I took a look at the Pill she was taking each day—M & M's!

I married a girl who's crazy for pickles and ice cream. I'll never forget how I first learned she was pregnant. She woke up in the middle of the night and had this mad, craving for a glass of water!

Did you hear about the wife who was so frigid, she was arrested on her honeymoon? For indecent composure?

I don't wanna complain about my wife, but in Alaska they just named a glacier after her!

You may have heard of my wife—Frigid Bardot?

WIFE—CLEANING

My wife is so neat, when she makes up her mind she uses hospital corners.

My wife has tried every detergent, soap powder, soap flake, soap liquid ever made—and she's finally found the one thing that's kindest to her hands—the phone, when she calls a laundry to pick it up!

My wife just brought home the greatest washday miracle of them all—a maid!

Remember when wives used to spend all their spare time mending socks? Now they don't give a darn!

My wife doesn't mind cooking, cleaning, washing, and scrubbing the floors—ever since she discovered the greatest household helper of them all—tomorrow!

My wife has a wonderful way of keeping all her dishes and pots and pans sparkling clean. She never uses them.

I made a big mistake when I put my wife on a pedestal. Now she can't reach the floor to clean.

My wife finally got around to spring cleaning. I say "finally" 'cause the first thing she picked up from the floor was tinsel.

Her biggest problem is dusting. Every day people come in and flip over our gray wall-to-wall carpeting—and we don't have any!

That's what our living room looks like. Wall-to-wall gray dust. It looks like an old cotton field!

It all started innocently enough. She asked me: "What's on the television?" And I said: "Dust!"

She said: "I'll have you know I dust once a week!" I said: "Oh yeah? So how come the roaches in the kitchen are gray?"

You have no idea. Last week *Good Housekeeping* bought back her subscription!

WIFE—CLOTHES

Have you ever noticed the way women keep the best things in life for themselves? Like, when has your wife ever asked you to button up the *front* of her dress?

My wife isn't talking to me this week. Last Friday she's wearing a $30 paper dress—and I'm trying to train a puppy. So I said: "On the paper!"

For years my wife has been complaining she has nothing to wear. I didn't believe her until she showed up in *Playboy* last month!

Did you read where women who take the birth-control pill are getting bigger bosoms? And if they don't take it, they're also getting bigger!

I heard these two women talking and one said: "I have a forty-inch bust and I owe it all to the pill." Her friend said: "What pill is that?" She said: "My husband. He makes falsies!"

Brassiere makers call it the Six Gun Syndrome. Women who used to have empty 32's, now have loaded 38's!

And if bosoms keep getting bigger, can you imagine the bra of the future? It won't be living—it'll be cantilevered!

I've even got a wonderful name for it: TWO MUCH!

Naturally, there's gonna be problems. If women get any heavier up front, that center page in *Playboy* is gonna fold out by itself!

Europeans claim American men are obsessed with U.F.O.'s and bras. That half the country is watching saucers and the other half is watching cups!

Frankly, I'm getting a little suspicious. I don't mind my wife wearing one of those tent dresses. It's those four feet sticking out the bottom!

WIFE—COOKING

She's the type who does all her own canning, preserving, and baking. Too lazy to go shopping.

A modern wife is one who spends the whole afternoon slaving over a hot stove—baking pottery!

My wife has come up with a wonderful new baking ingredient —flour and marijuana. She makes the only Ladyfingers in town that just lay there and snap!

I don't wanna say anything about my wife's cooking, but when she says: "Guess who's coming to dinner?"—it's an ambulance.

I've got a wife who's one of those modern cooks. Into every dish, she adds a little wine—a little rum—a little brandy. I don't wanna complain, but last night we had a fifth of pork chops!

I won't say what her cooking is like, but one day I sent her out for dinner and she burned the Diner's Club Card!

What some women don't know about cooking would fill a book. With her, it'd empty a package of Tums!

My wife is one of those imaginative cooks. Like you oughta see the way she times three-minute eggs. Cooks Minute Rice three times!

I'll say one thing for my wife's cooking. I've never been troubled by acid indigestion. If there's any acid, her food dissolves it!

My wife cooks soul food. Tastes just like a shoe!

My wife has only one problem with cooking—she burns things. Like we were married three years before I realized there were other flavors besides charcoal!

But I'll say one thing. My wife has come up with a wonderful device to keep food costs down. It's her cooking!

You know how some dinners end up with a demitasse and a cordial? In our house, it's a phone call and a stomach pump!

WIFE—HAIR

But the latest word from the fashion world is that teased hair is going out. In all directions!

My wife has teased hair, and it looks irritated.

Yesterday she came home from the beauty parlor, whipped off her babushka and said: "What does it look like?" I said: "A bleached nest!"

And every time I try to kiss her, she says: "Please! Don't muss the hair!" Do you realize what this does to a fella? She's sexy and I'm celibate!

My wife's been using one of those shampoos with a beer base, and it's fascinating. She doesn't put her hair up in curlers—in pretzels!

My wife walks around with so many curlers in her hair, yesterday a Martian walked up her and said: "Take me to your— Forget it. I'm looking for one of *them!*"

And these things are dangerous. Like I just figured out how Van Gogh lost that ear. His wife slept with pin curlers!

My wife happens to be a natural blonde. I know. It says so on the bottle!

WIFE—MONEY

I won't say how long I've stood in front of department stores waiting for my wife to come out, but yesterday a motorcycle cop put a chalk mark on my leg!

I don't mind my wife trying to fill up her Green Stamp book, but she's emptying my checkbook to do it!

You have no idea the way my wife shops. She doesn't even have a charge-a-plate anymore. All she has to do is see a sale—and the goosebumps rise up in the shape of her credit number!

Spend? Last week she told me she bought a Renoir for $3000. And if you think I was upset at that point—you should have seen me when I found out it wasn't a sports car!

I just went through a terrible fiscal crisis. My wife devaluated my wallet.

WIFE—TEMPER

If Ralph Nader is really trying to stop things that can hurt you—how come he hasn't investigated my wife?

I won't say how my wife's been acting, but on St. Valentine's Day you ain't seeing me go near a garage!

I don't wanna say my wife is irritable, but they named a grass after her!

She's always got her mouth open. When we go to the beach she has tanned tonsils!

I don't know what's wrong with me. Every morning I wake up with this nagging headache—my wife!

Last night I had a terrible argument with my wife and words passed between us. I hit her with a book!

"I'm a massagynist."
"You mean a misogynist."
"No. My wife rubs me the wrong way!"

What every man needs is a little support, a little encouragement. Like I don't mind going off every morning into the rat race. I just wish my wife wouldn't bet on the rats!

Frankly, we only stay together because of the children. They're marriage counselors.

WIFE—WEIGHT

Boy, did I just get a scare! My wife came up to me and went: (ASSUME SEVERAL KARATE-TYPE STANCES, YELLING "YI!" WITH EACH ONE). I said: "Karate?" She said: "No. Tight girdle!"

Say, if you really wanna irritate your wife—tell her she ought to keep her girdles in the kitchen. She'll say: "Why should I keep my girdles in the kitchen?" Then you say: "Why not? They're potholders!"

I don't wanna brag, but I've got a wife who's halfway to being a sexpot. She's got the pot and she's working on the rest!

I wouldn't say my wife is fat. Let's just say she's a model—for duffel bags!

I think my wife is gaining a little weight. Yesterday we had to let out the sofa!

My wife's a hippie. Can't resist éclairs!

My wife loves sweets. Like, if she had been Eve in the Garden of Eden, the snake would have had to use chocolate layer cake!

She's the only woman I know who has to wear a stretch bathrobe!

They even wrote a TV show about her trying to get into a Volkswagen. It's called "Mission Impossible"!

WINTER

It's so cold in Mississippi the Ku Klux Klan is wearing thermal sheets!

And I'll tell you how cold Minnesota is. To people who live in Minnesota—Alaska is Miami Beach!

At night the temperature goes to 20 below zero. Kinda reminds me of my first wife!

Even in Miami it's freezing. Yesterday a bellboy held out his hand and got two things—a tip and frostbite!

New Hampshire in February is like a Siberia that's on our side!

You know why they don't have burlesque shows in New Hampshire? How would it look? A thermal G-string!

I always have the same problem in cold weather: How to get my car started in the morning and my wife at night!

WOMEN'S APPEARANCE

I once knew a girl who carried a flag in parades, and it's just awful what it did to her. She had the only belly button with an echo!

Did you read that report by clothing manufacturers that women are getting bigger in front? One lady didn't realize it until she bought a Volkswagen and had to let out the windshield!

If you don't think women are getting bigger, when was the last time you heard of one drowning?

Skinny? She's the only girl I know who has to keep her shoulder blades in a scabbard.

I just figured out why blondes have more fun. You can find them in the dark.

Isn't that a wild name for a beauty parlor? Curl Up and Dye?

Thanks to pin curlers, ten million American women have flat noses—from sleeping on their face!

Women are obsessed with these pin curlers. I know a woman who wore pin curlers for her operation—so she'd look good for the autopsy!

WOMEN'S CHARACTER

This girl is so pure, she'd be considered a fanatic in the Virgin Islands!

I don't wanna say anything about my girl friend, but when it comes to the sexual revolution—a Pancho Villa she ain't!

Dull? She'd have to go topless just to be a wallflower!

I once had a girl friend who was an after-dinner speaker. Every time she opened her mouth, she was after dinner.

Lemme describe this girl to you. She would never leave lipstick all over a martini glass. Over a beer can, maybe!

She's the shy, demure type. Only looks for one thing in a man— a rich father.

Did you hear about the girl who went on a yachting party and hated herself in the mooring?

You gotta be careful of women. I know a wife who found out her husband had four girl friends all told. That's how she found out.

She's the type who's easy to look at. Never pulls down the shades.

She's the type who believes in early marriages. Her last three were before noon.

She's the friendly type. The kind you can have a wonderful evening with—even if you play your cards wrong.

Has this girl been around? She knows six house detectives by their first knock.

She's crossed more state lines than Greyhound!

She's the type who never wants to go too far—'cause if you park right away, there's more time.

Hippies want to love everybody. I once had a girl friend who wanted to love everybody. Her problem was, she was doing it one person at a time!

She's the type of housewife who always puts off today what the maid can do tomorrow.

WOMEN'S CLOTHES

It's amazing how many women are wearing dresses and sweaters with nothing underneath. It's called The Irish Look—Erin No Bra!

Not that wearing a sweater with nothing underneath is anything new. Twiggy's been doing it for years!

Fashion designers say that any girl who goes without a bra is a swinger. And if she's a 38, you better believe it!

One look at these styles and you think Minsky opened a boutique!

Personally, I blame the no-bra look on the Communists. It's just a sneaky way to make Russian women look chic!

As usual, it's the chubby women over forty who are gonna have trouble with this style. One of them took off her bra and almost killed a midget!

Do you realize what all these no-bra sweaters and mini-skirts are doing? It's been six months since any man has looked a woman in the eye!

You can't even call this fashion. It's nudism on the installment plan!

Isn't it interesting how just a few words can tell an entire story? Like the girl who got a maternity mink coat?

It's unbelievable how times have changed. I just saw a full-page ad for hostess pants. Hostess pants! Twenty years ago the only time you ever got to see hostess pants was if you were the host!

I think we owe a lot to nudism. Thanks to nudism we finally know why women's slacks are so tight!

Personally, I don't approve of girls wearing these big black boots. Yesterday I followed a pair for three blocks and it was embarrassing. It was a fisherman!

Now there's a girdle that's made from old automobile parts. It's called a Ford Foundation.

WOMEN'S DRESSES

And those gowns women are wearing. I tell you, they're enough to give you the peeps!

The big thing this year is the Peek-A-Boo Dress. That's a dress that isn't all there for women who are.

One dress is cut out so that you can see the navel. I don't know how sexy this is, but you'll always be able to tell who carries the flag in parades!

Have you seen those paper dresses for women? Ain't that something—paper dresses? You don't have to worry about moths—termites!

They've got all kinds of paper dresses. One girl was wearing a crossword puzzle dress. I tried to fill it in, and did I get a cross word!

I'm a diplomat. My wife brought home one of these paper dresses, took it out of the bag and said: "What do you think?" I said: "It's lovely." She said: "That's the bag!"

Do you realize that some of these paper dresses cost $200? $200! It's cheaper to wear the money!

Naturally, there are some problems with paper dresses. Like, if you sit on a wicker chair in a paper dress, it's like a breakfast food. Shredded Seat!

And girls, if you wear paper dresses, don't smoke. 'Cause the ashes you drop on the floor may be your own!

I gotta tell you what happened to my accountant. His wife read about these paper dresses, and that night he comes home with a paper cut on his hand. . . . Well she gave him three things for it—Iodine, a bandage, and a divorce!

Have you seen these tent dresses the women are wearing? You don't know if they're exotic or expecting!

WOMEN'S MAGAZINES

Say, have you looked through any of the women's magazines lately? They're fascinating. It's like Peyton Place with recipes.

All day long housewives are reading articles like: HOW I CURED NAIL-BITING THROUGH PROMISCUITY. . . . THEY CALLED ME THE TEMPTRESS OF THE P.T.A. . . . WHY YOU SHOULDN'T HAVE AN AFFAIR WITH AN INTELLECTUAL: NOBODY LIKES A SMART ASSIGNATION! . . . BAWDINESS FOR BEGINNERS. . . . IS LSD FATTENING? . . . HOW TO BE POPULAR THOUGH PREGNANT.

They have one article by a new bride. It's called "What I Learned on My Honeymoon." She learned that husbands are just like the government. They promise a lot more than they can deliver!

And they're always running articles for women about the problem of the other woman. Believe me, men also have the problem of the other woman. Finding one!

It's marvelous the big words they use in these articles. Like "clandestine extra-marital cohabitation." Doesn't that have a ring to it? "Clandestine extra-marital cohabitation!" It almost makes you proud to be a part of it!

And if they don't use big words, they use euphemisms. Like: "My husband cheats on me!" What does that mean—cheat? You don't know if she should hide her purse or the maid!

But the advice is always the same: Discuss the problem with your family adviser. Personally, I've never met a family adviser. They're all off somewhere listening to dirty stories!

You can't even criticize these articles since they're all written by eminent medical authorities who write about sex dispassionately —'cause their hangup is money!

And these magazines are getting around. Yesterday a teacher caught a kid reading one of these women's magazines. He had it hidden in a copy of *Playboy!*

WORLD PEACE

I'll tell you how bad things are. You know those fellas who go around with signs saying THE END IS NEAR? I just saw two of them synchronizing their watches!

THE END IS NEAR! Sounds like the motto of the Playboy Club!

Isn't it a little discouraging to live in a world where if you're 99 years old, you might not see another war?

In summing up the world today, I know a fella who's building an ark—and no one's laughing!

I have a great idea to show the world we're truly humanitarian. It's a combination of napalm and Unguentine!

As the first step toward disarmament, they're gonna have to figure out a way to get the car away from my wife!

Did you ever get the feeling that in today's world, Attila would be considered a Dove?

I'm getting a little suspicious of one of the girls in the peace movement. She has this big sign saying: MAKE LOVE, NOT WAR— and there's a price on it!

I'm so peaceful, I'm not even antibiotics!

There's only one hope for this world—that do-it-yourself might extend to include thinking.

WORLD PROBLEMS

The problems of the world have become so complex even teen-agers don't have an answer.

I don't want to seem critical of our foreign policy, but sometimes I wonder if we don't have a leak in our think tank!

The world has so many problems, if Moses had come down from Mt. Sinai today—the two tablets he carried would be aspirin!

I just learned of a vicious new Communist plot to undermine the morale of Americans. They're spreading the rumor that "Dennis the Menace" is making it with "Little Orphan Annie."

The Peace Corps has a real problem in Africa. Like, I don't know of anyone who's gonna give up fertility rites for color TV.

Foreigners can't help but he impressed by our affluence. Why all over the world there are building shortages—while we have U. S. Information Offices to burn!

The International Communist Conspiracy has come up with a fiendishly clever plot to infiltrate every home in America. You hear this knock on your door and a voice says: "Ivan calling!"

Index